WHAT EVERY
SCHOOL
LEADER

NEEDS TO KNOW ABOUT RTI

.VIII.

Margaret Searle

WHAT EVERY SCHOOL LEADER

NEEDS TO KNOW ABOUT RTI

Alexandria, Virginia USA

1703 N. Beauregard St. • Alexandria, VA 22311-1714 USA
Phone: 800-933-2723 or 703-578-9600 • Fax: 703-575-5400
Web site: www.ascd.org • E-mail: member@ascd.org
Author guidelines: www.ascd.org/write

Gene R. Carter, *Executive Director;* Judy Zimny, *Chief Program Development Officer;* Nancy Modrak, *Publisher;* Scott Willis, *Director, Book Acquisitions & Development;* Genny Ostertag, *Acquisitions Editor;* Julie Houtz, *Director, Book Editing & Production;* Jamie Greene, *Editor;* Reece Quiñones, *Senior Graphic Designer;* Mike Kalyan, *Production Manager;* Keith Demmons, *Desktop Publishing Specialist;* Kyle Steichen, *Production Specialist*

Printed in the United States of America. Cover art © 2010 by ASCD. ASCD publications present a variety of viewpoints. The views expressed or implied in this book should not be interpreted as official positions of the Association.

All Web links in this book are correct as of the publication date below but may have become inactive or otherwise modified since that time. If you notice a deactivated or changed link, please e-mail books@ascd.org with the words "Link Update" in the subject line. In your message, please specify the Web link, the book title, and the page number on which the link appears.

PAPERBACK ISBN: 978-1-4166-0993-3   ASCD product #109097   n6/10
Also available as an e-book (see Books in Print for the ISBNs).

Quantity discounts for the paperback edition only: 10–49 copies, 10%; 50+ copies, 15%; for 1,000 or more copies, call 800-933-2723, ext. 5634, or 703-575-5634. For desk copies: member@ascd.org.

Library of Congress Cataloging-in-Publication Data
Searle, Margaret.
  What every school leader needs to know about RTI / Margaret Searle.
     p. cm.
  Includes bibliographical references and index.
  ISBN 978-1-4166-0993-3 (pbk. : alk. paper) 1. Remedial teaching. 2. School failure–Prevention. I. Title.
  LB1029.R4S43 2010
  372.43–dc22
                                    2010000500

20 19 18 17 16 15 14 13 12 11 10   1 2 3 4 5 6 7 8 9 10 11 12

WHAT EVERY SCHOOL LEADER

NEEDS TO KNOW ABOUT RTI

Preface

The RTI framework coordinates the best of what we know about assessment, research-based instruction, intervention, and the kind of collaboration that breeds quality programs. When I first read the RTI regulations, they made me do my little happy dance because of their simplicity and commonsense approach. Finally, there were some guidelines powerful enough to make a difference but open-ended enough to allow each school district to tailor the implementation to its own needs.

As I consult with districts to help them formulate and implement school improvement plans that include RTI requirements, I hear the same comments over and over. Administrative and teacher leadership teams want to know:

- Where should we start?
- Where do I find research-based interventions?
- What's a pyramid of interventions and who can show me what to put in the tiers?
- If this means more testing, how are we going to have any time to teach?
- How is this whole thing going to work without killing us?

Some of these answers are relatively simple because RTI is built on a solid foundation of best practice. I often suggest strategies I have used myself as a teacher, supervisor, and principal to help teams see that quality practices and programs they've implemented in the past fit nicely into the RTI framework.

As I search to find practical and effective ways to support teachers and students, I continue to learn about wonderful books, Web sites, articles, and resources. Each provides helpful ideas, but, unfortunately, I haven't been able to find anything that puts all the RTI pieces (quality assessment, research-based instruction and intervention, and collaborative problem solving) together for both elementary and secondary schools. That is my mission in the following pages.

In this book, I attempt to paint a broad picture of the separate RTI components and how they fit together. At the same time, I will help you link these RTI components to all the great work already done in your district and school. RTI, thankfully, is not a new initiative or a program you can buy. It is simply a framework in which educators organize and coordinate what they have in place and then identify and fill in the missing pieces. If your district has been working on differentiation, summative and formative assessments, research-based interventions, professional learning communities, inclusive education, 21st century skills, mapping, and self-monitoring, you're already ahead of the game. All of these initiatives fit within the general RTI structure.

In Chapter 1, we look at the "big picture" behind RTI and the student-centered thinking behind the legislation. We will begin to connect the dots between quality programs already in place and the new responsibilities that RTI demands. Your job will be to identify gaps between these "dots" and opportunities to upgrade your system without sacrificing the valuable work that came before. There is always a need to progress to the next level of excellence.

Who isn't tired of starting new programs that sound great in theory but are then pulled up by the roots before they have time to flower? That is an exhausting waste of time, energy, and resources. It's time for all educators to get serious about the effort they devote to new improvement plans. RTI calls for a systemwide commitment, with all the resources and administrative support that entails. In Chapter 2, we learn how to set up this infrastructure that will ultimately support, focus, and sustain your RTI goals.

RTI requires a higher-quality assessment system than most initiatives by blurring the line between assessment and instruction. The process focuses on the use of data in decision making, not on data collection to simply comply with regulations. Through pertinent examples, we examine the "how" and "why" of assessment in Chapters 3 and 4.

Chapters 5 and 6 describe the pyramid of interventions and ways to build capacity in your staff. Options must be in place that provide the type of evidence-based instruction and interventions that are helping schools across the nation deliver better results. We discuss the three tiers of intervention and ways to design and implement them. We also take a close look at powerful methods to strengthen Tier 1 classroom instruction so that it minimizes the need to overuse more costly and labor-intensive Tier 2 and Tier 3 interventions.

RTI depends on teamwork for success. If teachers are asked to "go it alone," quality goes down and frustration goes up. Chapter 7 describes a step-by-step problem-solving process that supports staff and parents when they get stuck. Through early interventions and coordination of programs and resources, many students who were formerly misidentified with a learning disability can receive appropriate supports within a general education setting.

Chapter 8 puts all the pieces together and helps you plan a road map for moving forward. Are you ready? Let's get started.

Acknowledgments

There is no way for an author to write without drawing from a wealth of people who are willing to share their wisdom and provide encouragement. Many thanks go to all the schools who were willing to try new ideas and share tried-and-true ones. The questions you asked, the deep caring you showed for your students, and the problems we solved together helped refine and develop the ideas in this book.

I am especially indebted to Sycamore Community Schools in Cincinnati, Ohio for allowing me to be a partner in their day-to-day celebrations and struggles as they implemented the RTI process over several years. This experience has been worth its weight in gold.

Many thanks to my valued friends and partner consultants Dr. Karen Ackerman-Spain, Joan Love, Deb McDaniel, Marilyn Swartz, and Dr. Mary Jane Roberts for all the late-night problem-solving and brainstorming sessions that added so much to the clarity of this book and my energy to write it. A special thanks to Deb Siegel, from Solon City Schools, and Genny Ostertag, from

ASCD, for providing the most thorough and insightful critiques an author could possibly wish for. Keeping me on track and between the lines is no small task.

My deepest gratitude goes to my husband, Michael, and my two fantastic children, Morgan and Kenton, for putting up with my marathon sessions in front of the computer while they made the chaos of getting ready for college, doing homework, and completing chores seem like smooth sailing (when I know just the opposite was often true). Michael provides the inspiration that keeps me moving forward when it seems there is no end to the work. Morgan, Kenton, and their friends keep me focused on how important it is to make the school environment safe and welcoming for students if we truly want them to learn well and continue to love learning throughout their lives. I thank them all.

1

What Is RTI and
Why Should We Care?

"I am at my wits' end. Jerry is having a tough time with geography even though he is more than capable of doing the work. In fact, I have four students who are in the same boat. I call their parents, but these kids still won't do the work. It's obvious they don't get much help at home. Personally, I think it's a bad case of laziness. Why weren't they tested earlier? If I refer them now, they probably won't qualify for anything. I guess there's nothing to be done."

Does this sound familiar? Many teachers lounges are buzzing with conversations just like this. Accepting these types of situations as status quo is not only frustrating but also unproductive. Wouldn't it be more satisfying for this teacher to have a menu of solid instructional options from which to choose rather than rely on a referral process that she suspects will go nowhere? Wouldn't it save a lot of work and exasperation if she could talk to colleagues about relevant current research and instructional approaches that work with students who aren't inspired to apply the ability they already have? Wouldn't the school system work more efficiently if all teachers had a problem-solving framework to help them quickly respond to students' needs without clogging up the system with needless testing and inappropriate placements? Wouldn't developing an action plan at the first signs of trouble be more productive than spending time blaming other teachers or parents? A well-implemented Response to Intervention (RTI) plan addresses these issues and much more.

The Three Basics of a Quality RTI Plan

I have found it helpful to envision the RTI framework as a three-legged stool. The three legs are (1) an assessment process, (2) a tiered intervention menu, and (3) a problem-solving process. Each leg of this stool must be in place for the framework to be stable and functional (see Figure 1.1).

Figure 1.1 | **Representative Structure of the RTI Process**

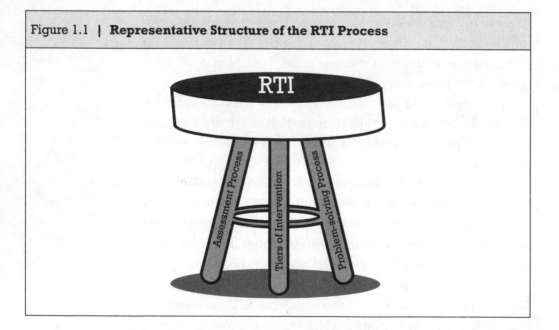

The first leg of the stool is the heart of RTI. Just as feedback helps runners shave seconds off their time, educators and students need specific data to stay on target and make appropriate adjustments if the going gets rough. The RTI process uses data from three assessment tools (discussed in further detail in Chapters 3 and 4) to meet this objective.

1. Universal screening data help pinpoint high-priority areas of concern. Screening provides data that help answer fundamental questions: What should we keep and what needs to be dropped or updated? Which students are in danger of falling through the cracks if we do not intervene quickly?

2. Diagnostic assessments refine the universal screening data by identifying the root causes for gaps between expected outcomes and actual performance.

3. Progress monitoring provides continuous feedback about how successfully the selected intervention is promoting student growth and closing achievement gaps. It also helps determine when a change in strategy is required.

Three levels of assessment drive the RTI process: universal screening, diagnostic assessment, and progress monitoring.

The second leg of the RTI stool provides a continuum of research-based interventions. It does no good to pinpoint which students need support if, once identified, there is no help available to find solutions. Teachers need access to a menu of research-based possibilities, ranging from whole-class strategies to more intense individual interventions that require special training to implement. Typically, intervention categories are arranged into a three-tiered pyramid (see Figure 1.2), which will be elaborated on in Chapters 5 and 6.

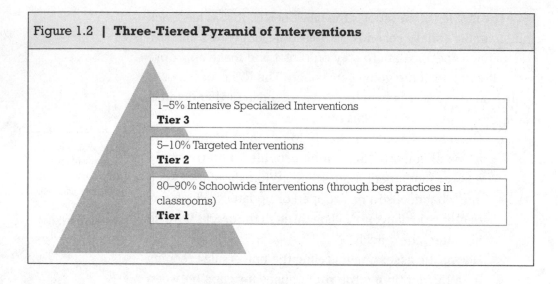

Figure 1.2 | **Three-Tiered Pyramid of Interventions**

1–5% Intensive Specialized Interventions
Tier 3

5–10% Targeted Interventions
Tier 2

80–90% Schoolwide Interventions (through best practices in classrooms)
Tier 1

- Tier 1 provides research-based classroom instructional strategies powerful enough to enable 80–90 percent of students to be successful without further intervention.
- Tier 2 provides interventions of moderate intensity that supplement Tier 1 strategies and are provided for groups of three to six students. Five to 10 percent of students may need assistance at this level.
- Tier 3 provides intense interventions provided for groups of one to three students. Like Tier 2, this level is also a supplement to Tier 1, not a replacement for it. One to 5 percent of students generally need assistance at this level.

The problem-solving team uses the intervention pyramid to help teachers and families identify appropriate solutions.

The final leg of the RTI stool is an efficient problem-solving process, often referred to as an Intervention Assistance Team (IAT) or a Student Support Team (SST). This component uses data from the assessment cycle to prescribe, monitor, and adjust intervention plans. Think of it as the support system that makes the assessment and intervention legs of the stool functional and efficient. This process will be explained further in Chapter 7.

RTI: What It Is and What It Isn't

RTI is a systematic way of connecting instructional components that are already in place. It integrates assessment data and resources efficiently to provide more support options for every type of learner.

RTI *does*

- Develop a systematic way of identifying student strengths and weaknesses.
- Reduce the time students wait to receive necessary instruction and intervention.
- Require schools to ensure that underachievement is not due to a lack of appropriate instruction.
- Require close monitoring and documentation of student responses to research-based instruction in general education classrooms, so schools are less likely to label students too quickly.
- Require that general and special education classrooms share responsibilities to ensure that all students can receive additional support using a seamless instructional system.
- Require the use of research-validated practices in core classroom instruction and supplemental intervention services.

RTI *does not*

- Apply only to students who qualify for special education.
- Allow students to wallow in failure until they meet a qualification score.
- Focus more on compliance to forms and procedures than on student results. It does promote procedures that get the right services to the right students at the first signs of trouble.
- Ignore the bias of assessment instruments that overidentify students who lack prior knowledge due to

environmental and cultural differences that are easily misinterpreted as a learning disability.

- Simply refer, test, and label students when they underperform in general education classrooms without proving that the problem is not the fault of the curriculum or the instruction.

The Two Models of RTI

There are two RTI models, and both have the same basic requirements.

There are two models for implementing RTI: the standard protocol model and the problem-solving model. Though there are pros and cons for each model, they both follow the same treatment cycle. Teachers must

- Assess all students with a universal screener.
- Diagnose reasons for any problems flagged by the screener.
- Select research-based interventions for the specific problems identified.
- Implement the selected plans and monitor them for positive effects.
- Adjust intervention plans in response to the progress monitoring and diagnostic data collected.

The protocol model

The protocol model prescribes a very specific intervention for all students who exhibit similar problems and fall below an established districtwide benchmark. This intervention is based on scientifically validated research and is the only intervention plan used to solve the identified problem. The staff implementing this intervention is carefully trained and regularly monitored for fidelity of implementation (i.e., implementation consistent with the research).

The advantages of the protocol model are	The disadvantages of the protocol model are
• More efficient staff training that focuses on only one research-based intervention plan for a given problem area. • A highly standardized program that allows relatively easy fidelity monitoring. • A predetermined intervention that reduces team meeting time.	• The limitations of only one approach, which may not accommodate the needs of every learner. • A potentially weak buy-in from staff charged with implementing a plan they have had no hand in developing or selecting. • Limited staff training on a variety of research-based approaches.

The problem-solving model

The problem-solving model relies on a team of experts who customize intervention plans to suit individual learners' needs. Team members must be trained to analyze the strengths and needs of learners and the teachers who instruct those learners. This careful analysis, performed before an action plan is created, prevents the loss of precious time caused by implementing the wrong interventions. Team members draw from a broad array of research-validated interventions and assessment tools.

The advantages of the problem-solving model are	The disadvantages of the problem-solving model are
• Customized plans that are appropriate for both learners and educators. • A flexible model that can be adapted to individual students' needs. • A potentially strong buy-in from those who implement the plan, resulting from their direct input.	• The requirement that team members possess a high level of expertise in many areas. • More time-consuming training and intervention design. • The difficulties in monitoring such a fluid process.

A 2008 study conducted by the Special Education Leadership and Quality Teacher Initiative found that 24 of 42 responding state departments of education recommended a combination of the two intervention models (Hoover, Baca, Wexler-Love, & Saenz, 2008). With a dual approach, students receive the customized plan provided by the problem-solving model while ensuring

A combination of models works best.

that the strategies selected come from a list of research-based interventions called for by the protocol model.

What RTI Looks Like When Done Well

As I work with educators to create their RTI plans, I notice that common themes tend to run through their comments and questions regarding the RTI framework. The following sections, introduced by representative comments, illustrate the core characteristics of a properly executed RTI plan.

Shared roles and responsibilities

Randy, a middle school intervention specialist, asked, "Why do general education teachers need to be involved with RTI training and implementation? I always thought RTI was just a new way to determine eligibility for students with disabilities. Isn't that the job of the psychologists and special education teachers?"

This is the first time special education legislation has as much impact on general education as on special education. In most schools, the new procedures for eligibility are a small part of the RTI plan. RTI is intended to deliver a wider variety of general education options before the words *special education* are even uttered. Only when Tier 1 interventions fail to close learning gaps do more intensive services—including English as a Second Language, gifted education, remedial classes, and tutoring—come into play. These services are supplementary to interventions begun and maintained by general educators. The goal of RTI is to prevent problems for all students; as a consequence, major shifts in roles and responsibilities are often necessary at all levels.

RTI began as a response to a 30-year argument about the best and worst ways to decide upon eligibility for special education services. Early in the process, there was little consistency among districts about what constituted a Specific Learning Disability. In response to this dilemma, a discrepancy formula was developed to determine whether a student's actual achievement was significantly different from his or her predicted achievement based upon his or her IQ score. It didn't take long for educators to question the wisdom of this formula. Though it was easy to calculate and helped with consistency, there were three serious negative side effects.

The discrepancy model didn't demonstrate a big enough gap between achievement and ability for young children to qualify for services until they reached the 3rd or 4th grade. This often resulted in the "sorry, we'll have to wait until you're far behind your peers" response. Students' needs were overlooked or ignored until they were considerably behind their peers, and only then were services provided. Research has shown that early interventions are more powerful and effective than those applied after the problem has become deeply rooted, yet this delay was common practice.

The Individuals with Disabilities Education Improvement Act (IDEIA) now requires that students both with and without disabilities are provided with proactive, supplemental support as soon as a teacher detects a potential difficulty. Regulations regarding early intervention services (EIS) permit schools to use up to 15 percent of the district IDEIA Part B funds to develop and implement EIS.[1]

> IDEIA requires that all students be provided with supplemental support as soon as a difficulty is detected.

Another downside of the discrepancy formula was its bias in the assessment of students from culturally and linguistically diverse backgrounds. Many students who could have succeeded with far less intensive services were mislabeled. Even though "rule outs," such as cultural background, socioeconomic circumstances, and lack of appropriate instruction, are built

---

[1] The requirements for EIS are found in the regulations at 34 CFR §300.205(d), 300.208(a) (2), 300.226, and 300.646(b) (2).

A disproportionate number of African Americans, English language learners, and children from disadvantaged socioeconomic circumstances are misidentified as disabled.

into the law, these safeguards were generally ignored in an effort to provide assistance to struggling children. As a result, a disproportionate number of African Americans, English language learners, and children from disadvantaged socioeconomic circumstances were identified as disabled. The RTI process, however, decreases misidentification by providing options that are less intensive than special education.

The eligibility assessment procedures formed the crux of the third problem with the discrepancy formula. Even though the regulations call for "multifactored evaluations," the information typically collected is more helpful for sorting and labeling students than it is for designing specific programs. Even though the regulations call for "appropriate educational programs," studies suggest that many achievement and behavior problems are actually due to shortcomings in both general and special education instructional programs (National Research Center on Learning Disabilities, 2007).

Trying a variety of approaches before referring students to special education should have always been the first step, but many districts subscribed to the mentality that "if the student doesn't fit, refer him, test him, and dispatch him to someone else's program." Schools need to shift this old paradigm to a new RTI way of thinking, though this will likely require significant cultural changes. With an RTI approach, psychologists and specialists focus their time on designing interventions rather than checking for eligibility.

Increased progress monitoring

Progress monitoring helps teachers know when to change strategies.

Lynn, an elementary school principal, asked, "What is this watch list I keep hearing about? How are these students identified and who needs to watch them?"

A watch list is a list of potential struggling learners identified by district universal screening procedures. Teachers typically monitor these students on a weekly or biweekly basis, using progress monitoring probes to gauge the success of selected interventions. If student growth data are weak, teachers should immediately change strategies rather than wait until a student is in trouble or qualifies for a label. In strong RTI buildings, teams take genuine pride in helping students move off the watch list. You can feel a sense of personal challenge ignite team spirit and morale, with a common sentiment being, "We've saved another one from slipping through the cracks!"

Coordination of support and resources

Darcy, a curriculum director in an urban district, stated, "RTI makes so much sense to me because it coordinates every program, resource, and service into the three-tiered intervention model. This makes our old practice of adding programs and services that all worked independently look like a disjointed mess. How do schools get this job done?"

Teachers often recognize the disconnect between general education and the myriad special education resource services. They are happy to have students receive help but are frustrated when those students are constantly pulled out of class for tutoring and other services. If the focus of core and intervention classes matched, students wouldn't miss critical instruction. They would receive a double dose of the same skills that were taught using different approaches and from a variety of teachers. Strong curriculum maps, flexible schedules, common planning times, and efficient communication are the key elements to this type of coordination.

Coordination among general education and special education support services is essential.

Team problem solving

Olivia, a school psychologist, said, "When I first heard that the RTI framework needed a problem-solving team, I thought, 'Well, here is a place where our district is already on target.'

What I learned, however, knocked my socks off. Now we need to involve students and families in the team meetings every time. How do you get them to participate?"

Families and school personnel need to share responsibility for student improvement. Often, this home/school cooperation doesn't happen because the school does not provide a safe and welcoming environment for families experiencing problems. The magic behind an RTI problem-solving meeting is the rule that states, *There will be no admiring or even talking about the problems during the meeting.* RTI problem-solving meetings with families are strictly for creating action plans that solve the pre-agreed-upon problems. The policy of not blaming others or describing student problems dramatically changes the dynamics so that every participant feels encouraged and supported, rather than attacked and defensive. This approach makes the team meeting environment 100 percent safe and welcoming for the student, family, and school personnel involved.

Focused leadership

Ken, a superintendent of a small rural district, made this observation: "My 'ah-ha moment' was seeing how visibly the superintendent and the principals must lead this effort every single day. Where do we start?"

Select a few high-priority areas and attend to them daily for at least two to three years if you want the change to become common practice. Without clear priorities, the initiative will weaken and look like a "flavor of the month." Teachers are quick to spot half-hearted improvement efforts and will often take a "this too shall pass" attitude. Regularly discussing data and strategies keeps the energy, resources, and talent moving in a unified direction. Chapter 2 will go into more detail about how both administrators and teacher leaders typically set up and maintain effective RTI structures.

RTI Changes Our Thinking

The following dialogue between two teachers addresses some common concerns and thoughts about how RTI impacts the school improvement effort.

Renee: Let me see if I understand this. RTI is a new type of prereferral to determine eligibility for special education services, right?

Matt: Yes and no. Eligibility is a small part of the RTI process. A primary purpose is to increase options within general education without going through the hassle of a formal referral. You may refer students later if the interventions don't work, but no time is wasted in the meantime. RTI strives for immediate support for students.

Renee: That sounds like it could delay students with legitimate disabilities from receiving services.

Matt: RTI cannot deny or delay a formal evaluation for special education. At any point in an RTI process, IDEIA 2004 allows parents to request a formal evaluation to determine eligibility. However, we won't wait for the test results to start helping students. Do you remember when we used to refer a student and then wait months only to find out that he didn't qualify for anything? How frustrating was that? Now we can provide interventions while we evaluate the need for a multifactored evaluation. RTI is less about labeling and more about getting appropriate services to students as quickly as possible. Generally speaking, referrals, once made, don't require as much time because

A primary purpose of RTI is to increase options within general education.

RTI cannot deny or delay a formal evaluation for special education.

data collection has already begun through the RTI process.

Renee: RTI sounds like another set of hoops for special education teachers to jump through.

Matt: RTI requires general, remedial, gifted, and special educators to collaborate as they plan, deliver, monitor, and adjust interventions within the general education setting first. If everyone involved doesn't plan and work together, then the system will likely fail.

Renee: Well, good luck with that. This sounds like a lot to put on already full plates. Where are we going to find the time and resources to do all of this?

Many existing programs and services fit into the RTI model.

Matt: We already have several of the RTI components in place. We just haven't called it RTI. We have aligned our curriculum and chipped away at differentiated instruction for years. We practically eliminated tracking and replaced it with flexible grouping. Kids with IEPs have higher expectations and are learning with their nondisabled peers more than ever before. All of this is part of the RTI infrastructure. However, identifying more time to plan together is a must, and there are some big assessment changes we will still need to tackle.

Renee: Oh, great, more testing. When am I supposed to teach these kids?

Matt: You're absolutely right; we need to drop some of our more labor-intensive tests and replace them with quick progress monitoring probes. That will actually save instructional time and provide more useful and timely information.

Renee: That sounds way too reasonable to actually happen, but I hope it works out that way. You know, research-based instruction is the other scary piece. How will I know how to implement research-based interventions? Where do I find those ideas?

Matt: It used to be difficult, but there are a lot of materials and many Web sites now available. We need training. We also need fidelity monitoring to reassure teachers that they are implementing the plans in the most effective manner.

Renee: That sure beats crossing our fingers and hoping that we're doing the intervention correctly.

Matt: Our intervention teams will also use some new protocols to upgrade our services. Problem-solving teams will focus on student data to help teachers set specific learning targets before designing and adjusting interventions and services. We will no longer just admire the problems and label students. Problem solving will also be more collaborative as we coordinate the efforts of the student, his or her family, and a variety of faculty members.

> RTI requires research-based interventions.

Where Did RTI Come From?

Over the past 30 years, special education laws and revisions have been criticized, analyzed, and adjusted, but the mandates needed to trigger significant change did not appear until the reauthorization of IDEIA 2004. The final regulations published in June 2005 are less about compliance and accountability and more about prevention and early intervention.

No Child Left Behind (NCLB) and IDEIA both require research-based models that include reliable screening and progress monitoring of student responses to evidence-based instruction. They also require the use of data to match instructional interventions to areas of specific student need as soon as those needs become apparent. The process must document that underachievement is not due to a lack of appropriate instruction.

RTI in Practice

RTI thinking applies to many levels of decision making, and effective results start with a systemwide application. After analyzing district data, leadership teams focus on the primary needs of the entire system. Individual schools then design action plans that apply district goals to their specific settings. Each department, grade level, and teacher then creates a plan to use these goals to meet the needs of individual students.

At every level, an established and proven sequence is followed to ensure that appropriate and timely decisions are made. This sequence includes the following steps:

1. District and building teams use data to create a priority-ranked list of issues in order to determine a few items for action.
2. Problem-solving teams use a diagnostic process to help unravel possible root causes of identified problems.
3. Clear, specific, and measurable goals guide implementation.
4. Teachers develop action plans shown to be effective by research.
5. Teachers carefully and frequently monitor individual student progress.
6. Teachers and administrators evaluate the adequacy of the RTI plan and make adjustments based upon this evaluation.

RTI at the district level

The leadership team at Insightful School District studied the data patterns from their K–12 universal screening results and the state testing scores from the previous year. The team identified two key issues that needed immediate attention.

1. Math scores were among the lowest in the county at every grade level, except grade 3—and that score was nothing to cheer about.
2. Students with disabilities and English language learners were identified as low-performing subgroups.

After establishing a districtwide improvement goal, the district council identified possible root causes for these issues, set two measurable goals, and developed a plan for monthly progress monitoring at the district level. They then realigned district resources to support individual building plans. Team members returned to their schools to involve staff in reviewing data and establishing their own continuum of interventions. Each building was charged with reporting its findings and progress to the district council on a monthly basis. This helped to coordinate the process and share the multitiered intervention plans across the district.

RTI at the building level

The Insightful School District high school faculty studied building data that targeted the district goals. The staff identified several math concerns unique to their school.

*   Many general education, special education, and ESL students were less than proficient with basic mathematical facts and were shaky on basic computation procedures.
*   The main instructional approach in 60 percent of math classes was a 30-minute "sit and get" lecture followed by independent work.

- Only 20 percent of staff used corrective feedback daily.

As a result of these findings, the math department created specific and measurable goals for the staff and their students. They contacted the county math supervisor for help with developing a research-based plan to meet their goals and measure their progress weekly.

The middle school faculty identified concerns similar to those acknowledged by their colleagues in the high school.

- Students demonstrated weaknesses in computation, especially with fractions, decimals, and percentages.
- Some teachers did not implement the curriculum map with fidelity, if at all.
- Weekly department meetings were needed to evaluate student progress data and make decisions about how to address students who were falling behind or required enrichment.

The middle school staff also established concrete goals in response to the identified concerns. Special education teachers and ESL tutors agreed to more coteaching to help with differentiation, and scores for both struggling and accelerated students would be charted and studied to monitor subgroup progress and make instructional changes as needed.

Each elementary school had a slightly different spin on why specific student progress was problematic. However, in response, they all

- Developed clear and measurable goals that resulted from the baseline data collected.
- Designed a research-based approach to reach their goals.
- Planned to measure and chart all students' progress monthly and "at-risk" students' progress weekly to gauge the success of the instructional methods used.

The Insightful School District superintendent instructed the district team to develop a method to display the monthly progress monitoring data so it would be easy for teachers to see how their efforts were paying off. Two separate sets of data were posted: one that showed math growth and one that showed ESL and special education progress in math and reading. All district buildings and the central office staff used these data to launch monthly discussions on how teams could support each plan and make adjustments to them.

Districts require data to gauge the effectiveness of plans and measure how well students and subgroups are progressing.

RTI at the grade and classroom levels

Based upon class data and district benchmarks, individual teachers designed classroom goals that contributed to the success of district and building goals. These classroom goals were the foundation upon which achievement of all other goals rested.

Let's visit Mrs. Wood's 5th grade classroom to see how this plays out. As Mrs. Wood considered the district's focus on math, the two areas of particular concern for 5th grade were math fluency and the application of math concepts. Class results from the universal screener on math fluency showed that

- Nine students rated poorly (0–8 digits correct per 2.5 minutes).
- Seven students rated close to goal (9–15 digits correct per 2.5 minutes).
- Eight students rated proficiently (16 or more digits correct per 2.5 minutes).

The universal screening data on the application of math concepts showed that

- Thirteen students rated poorly (0–5 blanks correct per 5 minutes).
- Six students rated close to goal (6–11 blanks correct per 5 minutes).

- Five students rated proficiently (12 or more blanks correct per 5 minutes).

Based upon these results, Mrs. Wood set a class growth goal to increase computation accuracy by an average of one digit each week and increase by .4 blanks correct per week for concepts for the following seven weeks. She prepared a graph to illustrate the current class average and where students would be in seven weeks if they worked together to meet this new goal. Her students were encouraged by the challenge and immediately decided that they needed a plan.

Students brainstormed strategies, and Mrs. Wood recorded their ideas on the board, pointing out that many of their ideas were also studied by universities and had made a big difference for most students. Mrs. Wood cautioned her students that they would only see a difference if they followed the strategies exactly as researchers designed them. The students decided to carefully monitor one another, and they invited the school principal to be their "second set of eyes"—to see if the research would really work for them. The class selected a peer practice strategy as the first intervention to be used for 18 minutes each day.

Mrs. Wood began by ensuring that every student understood the exact procedures for working with partners. Using different examples, she explained and modeled each segment of the peer practice strategy. Each student's folder contained a step-by-step set of directions and two sets of specially selected math flashcards with answers to the problems on the back. Mrs. Wood constantly walked around the room to watch and give feedback to students as they practiced together. She did not skimp on the amount of time spent teaching or reviewing the procedures because she understood that great ideas poorly implemented tend to cause problems that sacrifice precious instruction time.

Each district's issues and goals will be unique, but establishing and maintaining a systemic action plan is critical to a successful RTI framework. District and building leadership teams must set clear goals and keep everyone informed and focused by asking about data and intervention plans weekly. Teachers in all grades and subject areas need to coordinate their plans until the result is a seamless delivery of options that moves flexibly up and down the intervention pyramid.

Summary

RTI is not a program you can buy. It is not a pathway to special education. It is a method of organizing and coordinating school resources to create a more efficient range of options that serve all students in danger of not reaching their potential.

The spotlight on student learning is intended to create a culture of early intervention, thus putting to rest the old "wait-to-fail" model that delayed appropriate services. Early support is available to all learners, whether they are in a general education, special education, gifted, ESL, or another specialized environment. All students have access to a growing menu of options made possible by the coordination of resources and services.

Whether the protocol model, the problem-solving model, or a combination of the two RTI models is employed, faculty and families work together in new ways to provide academic and behavioral assistance. This necessarily requires rethinking roles and responsibilities at all levels.

Each of the following chapters provides specific steps and ideas to help you design and implement your own plan that will tap the strengths of your staff and meet the unique needs of your learners. In the next chapter, we will examine some guidelines for getting started and setting up a districtwide support system.

2

A Visible Means of Support

A great place to begin the RTI process is by building Tier 1 capacity.

Each school district with which I have worked approached RTI from a different perspective, implemented it for unique reasons, and made choices relevant to its specific circumstances.

One district began by training all middle and high school teachers on a different research-based strategy each month. After hearing several presentations—including "How to focus students in order to increase memory" and "How to increase motivation"—teachers developed methods to apply these ideas to their own classrooms. The leadership team used the monthly theme to focus classroom walkthroughs during the following 30 days. By the end of the first year, teachers recognized that Tier 1 classroom instruction was stronger and student motivation was better than ever before. It became obvious that, as teachers incorporated new strategies into their daily routines, the number of students needing intense interventions was reduced.

A school in a different district started the RTI process by revamping its Intervention Assistance Team. Meetings that once seemed ineffective and unproductive turned into shorter, more collaborative meetings that consistently resulted in concrete action plans. This new model involved parents and students as active participants. As a result, the staff saw significant changes in their students' willingness to assume responsibility for their own growth and development. In response, parents repeatedly described the new approach as a "breath of fresh air."

Ultimately, schools begin the RTI process in many different ways—ways that are unique to their specific issues and needs. They might focus on an individual building, selected grade levels, a single content area, or several subgroups of students. The bottom line is: there is not one universally correct place to begin, but there are definitely basic structures that increase long-term chances for success.

Great Leaders Make the Difference

One of the key differences between schools that approach RTI with passion and enthusiasm and those that tend to flounder is the leadership's ability to inspire people and maintain focus on a few priority issues. Rosalynn Carter said, "A leader takes people where they want to go. A great leader takes people where they don't necessarily want to go but ought to be." I have repeatedly witnessed the truth of this statement while working with schools that try to implement significant improvement processes such as RTI.

The following sections form an invaluable collection of insights from four leaders with whom I have worked over the years. Many of the lessons they share came as a result of "learning the hard way" and are offered as a gift from those who succeeded but may have borne more than their share of hardships along the way.

"A leader takes people where they want to go. A great leader takes people where they don't necessarily want to go but ought to be."

Following the leader

Dr. Sally Roth is the curriculum director in a small urban school district.

My advice is to have one committed and enthusiastic person present the long-term vision and short-term goals to everyone on staff. Do this as early as possible after the leadership team has a clear idea of where they need to begin. By having the same person articulate the big picture of what students need and why RTI is worth serious energy, we made certain that every group received the exact same message.

It was a huge advantage to do these presentations in small group settings with administrators present and involved. Training in groups of 25–30 gave all stakeholders the opportunity to ask questions, voice opinions, and give suggestions about how the vision might be implemented in their buildings. People were given time to reflect with their subgroups on how RTI would help them do a better job. They brainstormed ways to customize the plan for their specific situations. Administrators were able to hear concerns and support statements from their faculties early in the process. I think people left energized instead of drained because we gave them a full day to internalize and plan with their group.

HOW TO . . . *roll out the RTI framework*

- Help people see how they can use the RTI framework to address concerns they have had for years (e.g., Can we take some things off our plate to make room for more effective practices? How can we use our resources more efficiently? Are there more user-friendly ways of assessing student growth? How can we get parents and students more involved in problem solving?).
- Provide opportunities to try new procedures with real case studies.
- Tell engaging and informative stories to illustrate why and how the process works.
- Discuss ways to provide the time and support required for a successful RTI plan.
- Allow the option of in-depth training during the first two years, but make it clear that RTI is a priority and all staff are expected to participate within three years.

It is critical that the superintendent and principals lead an initiative for it to be taken seriously. In Sally's district, every principal attended the overview presentations and actively participated in the discussions. They did not bounce in and out of meetings, which would have spoken volumes about their lack of support. If the key administrators aren't the perceived leaders, then the likelihood of failure is very high, even when other talented administrators like Sally are doing an exceptional job.

How an administrator spends his or her time often points directly to immediate building priorities. I often hear, "I just can't spend the whole day in a seminar. I have discipline problems and other crises to deal with all day." Some administrators spend a majority of their time putting out fires, yet they spend comparatively little time establishing and nurturing programs and services that might potentially take the matches away from those setting the fires. In order to establish a culture of openness to change adult growth, the principal must be the most visible learner and participant in RTI implementation.

> The school principal must be the most visible participant in RTI implementation.

Granted, it is increasingly difficult to keep broad development goals in focus while the day-to-day "busyness" of school tends to sap enthusiasm and blur vision. However, regular one-on-one conversations—between the principal and individual teachers—about the schoolwide goals and student progress send a strong message that the district is planning to stay the course and that RTI is a top priority.

> Regular conversations between the principal and teachers indicate strong commitment to achieving schoolwide goals.

Charting a course

Ann Marie Reinke and Jennifer Manoukian are curriculum directors in a suburban district that has established many initiatives over the past several years.

> *Don't roll out RTI as a new initiative. Help people see how the RTI process honors work that has already been done and extends it to the next level of excellence. If you don't show the*

interconnectedness of past, present, and future efforts, you will hear complaints such as, "No more new programs! I'm already stretched too thin." You may hear some of that anyway, but showing RTI as a coordination and refinement of what is already working is one way to reduce feelings that the administration has foisted one more "random act of improvement" on people.

Simply adding to the mountain of work already expected of teachers and students cannot be expected to improve results.

In this particular district, the leadership team created a flowchart to illustrate how current programs, services, and initiatives would integrate into the new RTI process. At the same time, they also identified what could be replaced by more efficient programs and services.

Simply adding to the mountain of work already expected of teachers and students generally interferes with quality improvement efforts. Identifying and discarding less effective practices, programs, and initiatives is one of the toughest jobs of the RTI process, yet it is also one of the most essential. A considerable barrier to this process, however, is that most established programs and practices are somebody's "baby," and those people are understandably reluctant to let the group discard their plans. Gathering concrete data that analyze student growth for various programs helps move the discussion away from initial emotional responses.

Once the flowchart and list of programs to be discontinued is in place, it is a good idea to develop a timeline that illustrates three phases of implementation.

1. Past: accomplishments during the previous three years that support the RTI effort
2. Present: work required during the first year to firmly establish the RTI effort
3. Future: roles, responsibilities, and work required during the next three years to refine and maintain the RTI effort

Helping staff visualize the whole process and understand how implementation will be spread out over time also helps reduce the "panic factor." Choose Your Challenges is a good activity to promote and encourage staff buy-in.

ACTIVITY:	**Choose Your Challenges**
PURPOSE:	to help people connect what is already in place with the new process to rank identified problems by priority
MATERIALS:	- a Likert scale preassessment to rate issues under consideration for improvement - chart paper and a marker - visual timer to help groups pace their work
GROUP SIZE:	any size; subgroups should have no more than five
TIME:	30 minutes

PROCEDURE:

Step 1

After making a short—but inspiring—presentation on what research defines as essential components of a successful RTI program (inspiration is vital here), have teachers rate how well these RTI components are currently implemented at their school (never more than six components). Possibilities include universal screening, progress monitoring, intervention banks, problem-solving teams, and common time for teachers to analyze data and create action plans.

Teachers should then rate these components on a scale of 1–4, with 1 indicating "not typical" and 4 indicating "very typical." An elaboration of the ranking system might be:

1	We don't have this in place, or it is in place but completely ineffective.
2	We have this in place, but it is not implemented well or consistently.
3	We have this in place, and it is generally implemented well by everyone.
4	We could be a site for modeling this component to other buildings.

PROCEDURE (cont.)

Step 2

Allow the groups three or four minutes to rate the components, and then have them sequence the items from those in which they excel to those that need improvement. After five minutes, have each group present a two-minute report explaining their ranking and rationale. A moderator should record the rankings reported by each group.

Step 3

Have each small group discuss the top issues identified for improvement and then have the entire group decide upon and submit two or three tangible ideas for how to improve these components. Distribute a composite of possible action items to all staff later in the week to remind them of the part they now play in RTI planning.

The information gathered from this activity can be used throughout the planning and implementation stages to monitor progress and assure teachers that leadership groups are responsive to their ideas and feedback.

Figure 2.1 | **Example of a Likert Scale Preassessment**

Discussion Session
1 2 3 4   Teachers always leave IAT meetings with specific interventions that are different than what the teachers have already been doing.
1 2 3 4   Parents always leave with a specific plan of action for home.
1 2 3 4   Parents always leave feeling grateful and supported—never sad, blamed, or beaten up after an IAT meeting.
1 2 3 4   Teachers always feel grateful and supported—never blamed or attacked at IAT meetings.
1 2 3 4   Meetings always model these problem-solving steps: • We identify the root cause of the problem before we try to solve it. • We brainstorm multiple research-based ideas that fit the problem before we decide upon a plan of action. • We have a specific plan for collecting data to see if our plan is having a positive effect. • We follow up within six weeks to see if the data indicate success or a need to change the plan. • If the data are not positive, we modify the plan of action.
1 2 3 4   We always have a balance of accommodations and interventions that get *incrementally* more or less intense as we respond to our data.
1 = never true   2 = sometimes true   3 = generally true   4 = always true

IAT = Intervention Assistance Team

Leading the way

Adam McCray is the principal of a high school in a large urban district. As a veteran administrator, he has learned to adjust his leadership style by matching his behavior to what he knows about the stages of team development.

> *In the initial stages of our RTI process, I could see that the staff were reluctant to commit to anything. They had heard RTI war stories and had experienced many new "flash in the pan" ideas from our own district. Each panacea introduced was met with eye rolling and sidebar conversations; to tell you the truth, I really couldn't blame them.*
>
> *This time I wanted to start off in an entirely new way because I absolutely believe that RTI done well can be a turning point for us. Because they were in the "I'm not sure this is what we need" stage, I knew I had to start with their ideas for change and build our RTI plan around those expressed needs. Buy-in from at least a critical mass of people is crucial. The Keep or Cure activity was just the ticket I needed.*

It is almost universally recognized that a leadership style focused on pressure, blame, and ultimatums stifles creativity and commitment in nearly every environment. Simply encouraging people to try harder, when they are already working at or beyond capacity, rarely inspires anyone to go that extra mile. In fact, statements such as "They're not my kids" or "I'm not meeting with anyone during my planning time" are the common push-back responses many administrators face when they make the mistake of passing on their own stress.

Adam knew that lack of faculty ownership would reduce overall commitment to the process. He needed to organize people and help them collaboratively solve their own problems. He would not shove legitimate leadership responsibilities onto the heavily laden shoulders of his staff. He wouldn't ask teachers for decisions and then ignore or overrule their ideas if they didn't agree with his own.

Simply encouraging people to try harder, when they are already working at or beyond capacity, rarely inspires anyone to go the extra mile. Vision, support, and ownership are key ingredients to success.

Adam's sensitivity to the developmental needs of his faculty was pivotal to his success in getting the buy-in he needed early in the RTI process. Vague assertions about the bottom line only confuse people and delay the overall effort, so when the group didn't understand or agree with the district initiative, Adam was direct and clear about his expectations. He accomplished this by helping people link familiar, established programs with recognized priorities and the new task ahead of them.

Good leaders share power and authority for addressing issues that fall into everyone's area of responsibility. They create a sense of teaming for a worthy effort. They know that quality collaboration on important issues builds energy, even among very tired people.

The following activity helps form a cohesive whole among all participants by building on existing strengths, developing consensus on targeted areas of need, and encouraging teamwork to reach identified goals.

> Good leaders share power and authority. They understand that high-quality collaboration on important issues builds energy, even among very tired people.

ACTIVITY:	Keep or Cure
PURPOSE:	to recognize improvement efforts that have already worked to build commitment to work toward new objectives
MATERIALS:	- 3 × 3 in. sticky notes in two colors—enough to provide each person with two of each color - two large pieces of chart paper labeled "Keep" and "Cure" - brightly colored markers
GROUP SIZE:	any size
TIME:	30 minutes
PROCEDURE:	

Begin the activity by giving each teacher two sticky notes of each color—for example, yellow and blue. On each yellow note, have the teachers name one intervention option that is currently used to effectively help students experiencing academic trouble in general education classes. On each blue note, have them name a problem that needs to be addressed or something that needs to change in order to provide better student support. Teachers may fill out more than two sticky notes, but ensure that there is only one idea per note.

PROCEDURE (cont.)

After several minutes of brainstorming, ask teachers to post their yellow notes on the "Keep" chart and their blue notes on the "Cure" chart. As the meeting (and relevant discussion) progresses, have volunteers organize the notes on each chart into categories. Each category should be given a title that accurately describes the unifying idea.

Example categories for the "Keep" chart might include computer programs, before-school help, homework help, peer mentoring programs, and in-class assistance. It is refreshing and exhilarating to see how many programs are already in place to assist struggling students.

Example categories for the "Cure" chart might include a failure to complete homework, poor writing skills, scheduling problems, a need for individual assistance, a need to make up missing work, and poor note-taking skills. Usually, you can feel the group think "right on" or "absolutely" as the categories are read aloud and clarifying examples are given.

Finally, the group leader must connect the brainstormed ideas to the RTI framework. Explain how the "Keep" strategies and programs fit into the three-tiered bank of interventions. Then discuss how newly developed RTI approaches need to target the gaps identified on the "Cure" chart. You could be looking at

- Tier 1 strategies such as systematic instruction of note taking and writing in content areas.
- Tier 2 strategies such as computer-assisted practice and supplemental tutoring.
- Tier 3 strategies such as the addition of a second math period for students who require supplemental help beyond Tier 2 assistance.

By using the "Keep or Cure" activity, Adam was able to be direct and clear about expectations for the RTI improvement process right from the start. It provided a vehicle for building consensus around identified building needs, and it highlighted how the new plan built on existing programs and practices. The faculty also developed a sense of ownership in the new RTI initiatives. Adam's sensitivity to the developmental needs of his staff was pivotal in getting the commitment he needed early in the process.

Surround Yourself with Talent

The first step in building an infrastructure receptive to RTI thinking is to surround yourself with your district's best leaders.

District council and building leadership teams are necessary to guide and coordinate the process. The more that these groups accurately represent a variety of grades, roles, and areas of expertise, the easier it will be to maintain open communication and healthy collaboration. All administrators need to participate on the district council, and the participation of at least one enthusiastic and trustworthy building administrator is critical to each building leadership team.

Any lack of commitment, training, or willingness on the part of building principals can be a kiss of death. Carefully communicated expectations, insightful coordination, and dedication to progress monitoring are critical to RTI success. It is naïve to think that even exceptional teachers can independently develop and implement RTI without the consistent and visible support of dedicated administrators.

The Purpose of Leadership Teams

The job of all leadership teams is to cooperatively develop and implement a clear districtwide plan based on solid data. Providing teachers with a well-oiled support system reduces wasted time and considerable grumbling. The following is a "to-do list" for all teams charged with guiding the RTI process:

1. The district council targets one or two areas for improvement and sets measurable goals that are based on identified needs.
2. Building teams set their own goals, compatible with the larger district goals.
3. Building teams define specific membership roles and responsibilities to maximize coordination and minimize redundant and conflicting efforts.
4. The district council creates a monthly timeline that charts implementation, monitoring, and progress measurement.

5. Building teams create their own timelines, compatible with the overall district deadlines (see Figure 2.2).

6. Building teams meet monthly (at a minimum) to make decisions based on current progress data.

7. Teams at both levels provide and coordinate the use of technology, time, personnel, materials, and programs to help teachers achieve the goals.

8. Teams at both levels provide differentiated professional development to help teachers meet district and building goals.

9. The district council writes grants that support RTI efforts.

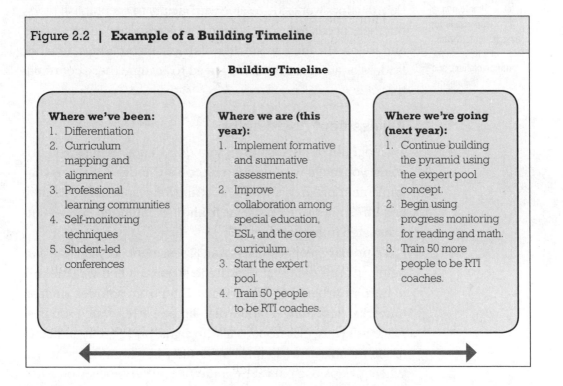

Figure 2.2 | **Example of a Building Timeline**

Building Timeline

Where we've been:
1. Differentiation
2. Curriculum mapping and alignment
3. Professional learning communities
4. Self-monitoring techniques
5. Student-led conferences

Where we are (this year):
1. Implement formative and summative assessments.
2. Improve collaboration among special education, ESL, and the core curriculum.
3. Start the expert pool.
4. Train 50 people to be RTI coaches.

Where we're going (next year):
1. Continue building the pyramid using the expert pool concept.
2. Begin using progress monitoring for reading and math.
3. Train 50 more people to be RTI coaches.

The Structure of Leadership Teams

There's an old saying that asserts, "If everyone is in charge, no one is in charge." Have you ever been on a team whose meetings gave entirely new meaning to *dysfunctional*? I have, and most of the time, the problem lay in leaderless committees and weak protocols. Successful leadership teams are communication links that provide essential support and resources to teachers. Obviously, teams function most efficiently when individual roles and responsibilities are clearly defined. Specific positions, and their related roles and responsibilities, are outlined in the following sections. Many times, these duties already form part of supervisors', counselors', and psychologists' job descriptions. Coordinators work side by side with faculty to accomplish tasks, but there needs to be one person who is responsible for closure and follow-through. In smaller districts or buildings, teacher leaders or administrators may need to assume these coordinator roles.

District and building RTI teams need coordinators responsible for assessment, pyramid of interventions, communications, and technology.

Assessment coordinator

Yogi Berra once said, "If you don't know where you are going, you might wind up someplace else." Indeed, districts that implement programs without setting very specific goals may end up "someplace else"—far from their intended goals—and exhausted from the effort.

A primary responsibility of an assessment coordinator is to help organize data that determine strengths and weaknesses of current programs and services. Data from sources such as universal screening, standardized tests, attendance reports, office referrals, classroom walkthroughs, and parent and community surveys are helpful to identify key areas of concern. When groups use relevant data to focus their energy on a few high-leverage goals, the result is often that many smaller problems disappear with little time or effort invested.

Building and district assessment coordinators help teams keep their focus by regularly compiling assessment data and displaying it in user-friendly formats. The assessment coordinator's main tasks are to

- Make recommendations for selecting universal screening and progress monitoring instruments that promote consistency throughout the district.
- Eliminate assessments and tests that are no longer needed.
- Help develop or purchase new assessment materials.
- Help develop and implement walkthrough procedures to monitor for fidelity of implementation.
- Oversee training that ensures consistent administration, assessment scoring, and walkthrough observations.
- Provide training to RTI problem-solving coaches in "five reasons" analysis (described further in Chapter 7) and progress monitoring.
- Collaborate with technology and media specialists to (1) implement computerized progress monitoring, (2) create user-friendly charts and graphs to easily facilitate data interpretation, (3) develop data storage and retrieval systems so information is easily accessible and transferrable, and (4) help teachers enter data into the district database.
- Assist with data analysis and interpretation by asking key questions that cut to the heart of the process.

What are some relevant questions that help identify meaningful patterns in the data?

- *What existing strengths can we build on and celebrate?*
- *What are the highest-priority problems for our system or building?*
- *Do some problems occur only at certain grade levels?*
- *Are some problems more pronounced in certain classes?*

- *How are our subgroups performing?*
- *What evidence indicates that we are using our time and talent wisely?*
- *Do community perceptions indicate high confidence in our schools?*
- *What type of professional development is needed?*
- *Which programs are yielding the highest success rate for student progress?*
- *Where should we focus our efforts and resources during the next three years?*

Once data have been collected and analyzed, assessment coordinators help the team limit action items to only two or three key concerns. I have seen teams decide to address every subject at every grade level, and, though it is a tempting and well-intended idea, this approach consistently leads to failed improvement plans. Let's face it, resources are limited and the more thinly these resources are spread, the less effective they will ultimately be. Attacking problems with laserlike precision—with the resources to effectively address the problems—yields considerably better results than the old "shotgun approach," where too many problems are targeted without the necessary support. Gradually phasing in improvement plans over several years is also essential to overall quality.

After helping teams set two or three challenging yet realistic goals, assessment coordinators need to establish progress-monitoring procedures that demonstrate two discrete sets of development data:

1. Evidence that the plan's implementation is conducted with quality and fidelity.
2. Evidence that the plan is having the desired effect on student growth.

Compose data teams to help teachers administer assessments and then chart and interpret the results. Too often, teachers simply collect and record student data; it should be a goal of the data teams to increase the focus on actually *using* this data to make instructional decisions.

Data teams generally include psychologists, counselors, literacy specialists, special education teachers, tutors, trained aides, college students, parents, students, social workers, building administrators, and central office supervisors. Obviously, team composition varies from school to school.

Teams of approximately seven members should be charged with the task of helping classroom teachers administer and score assessments. This relieves individual teachers of a potentially stressful burden. Instead of a single teacher tackling the assessment process for all of his or her students, administration time is dispersed among the team members. It should be noted that this process is done *with* the teacher and does not remove him or her. The teacher is involved at every step and always has the data. The team does not take the data but simply helps the teacher use it well. Technical, art, and media specialists can create user-friendly displays that highlight data patterns, helping teachers analyze critical data.

This approach has several advantages: (1) teachers benefit from modeling by other trained professionals, building their own skill and preciseness in the assessment process; (2) instructional time increases by reducing the teacher's workload and expediting classwide assessments; and (3) skills, expertise, and ideas are constructively shared in a cooperative setting.

Pyramid coordinator

No Child Left Behind and IDEIA 2004 require the use of research-based instruction and interventions, but accomplishing this is difficult. I have yet to meet a teacher who says, "I don't want to use researched strategies." However, I have met hundreds who ask, "Where in the world do you find that stuff?" This, then, is the primary duty of the pyramid coordinator: help staff members access a menu of research-based ideas and the assistance they need to implement these strategies and programs.

The main responsibilities of the pyramid coordinator include

- Organizing and leading staff efforts to identify research-based interventions.
- Developing a template that gives uniformity to the pyramid database, as described in Chapters 5 and 6.

- Merging the intervention strategies collected by individual schools into a districtwide electronic database. This will help teachers know who to contact for further information, guidance, and modeling of interventions that are new to them.
- Working with building administrators to ensure that adequate time, resources, and support are available to develop the database.
- Coordinating staff development.

HOW TO. . . *start a pyramid database*

The first step in developing a useful intervention database is to build on work that has already been done. Have the faculty list evidence-based programs and strategies that are helpful to students in the general education classroom (these are your Tier 1 programs and strategies). Filing these ideas by content area or problem addressed is helpful for retrieving information. Next, list the programs and strategies that can serve as "double doses" for students who need more time and corrective feedback than typical students in the general education classes (Tier 2). This extra help can be provided in either small-group instruction in the general education room or in other small-group settings such as study hall, intervention time, and Title I instruction. Finally, list the more intensive help offered for students who need daily specialized instruction in order to close the learning or behavioral gap (Tier 3). Intensive reading, writing, and math programs, double classes, gifted programs, and daily counseling sessions to build social skills are a few examples.

Creating this list together helps teachers see that RTI is not a new initiative, but an alignment and fine-tuning of current programs, skills, and practices. Once this inventory of current resources is complete, teams will be able to see where there are unmet student needs because of gaps in programs, strategies, materials, and training. Plans can then be made to fill these gaps by adding interventions or by realigning resources as each tier of the pyramid is developed and refined over the years.

One task of pyramid coordinators is to facilitate the development of each building's "expert pool" of resource people. (More detailed information on this process is described in Chapter 5.) This has proved to be a positive turning point for many buildings. In order to achieve buy-in for this important but intensive work, teachers must clearly understand the purpose and advantages of an intervention database and this particular method of creating one.

Teachers often ask, "Why doesn't someone just develop this for us?" If such an approach actually worked, there wouldn't be such a prevalence of weak intervention plans. Thousands of published books and programs describe a range of prescribed interventions, but people choose not to use them for a variety of reasons.

One reason is that teachers have limited time to search for all the research-based interventions they find themselves needing. If small groups specialize in one area of concern, like what to do about poor writing skills or how to help students who cannot stay focused, they can pool their expertise and become quick, personalized sources of quality interventions. Generally, teachers prefer to talk to peers who have tried a strategy instead of searching through books and Web sites for answers.

Another reason people don't actively search out interventions from prebuilt sources is that the "how to" and "what if" aspects of implementing unfamiliar strategies are seldom addressed in enough detail to be helpful. If a peer has already researched and tried a strategy, he or she is more capable of modeling the approach and guiding others through the appropriate steps.

Sometimes pyramid coordinators require a team of professionals to assist them with both professional development and the creation of a district intervention database. Members of the pyramid team often include literacy coaches, math and reading specialists, behavior specialists, community representatives, therapists, English language instructors, and technology coordinators. This group can also help administrators and assessment coordinators conduct fidelity monitoring of implementation (i.e., implementation that is consistent with the research).

Communication coordinator

Recently, as I was presenting RTI to a group of K–12 educators, one teacher announced, "You know, this RTI approach makes perfect sense. Why in the world hasn't our district gotten off the dime and started this already?" After several similar comments, one of the administrators explained that a district leadership team had, in fact, been working for over a year and someone should have been updating them. A rumble of side comments rippled through the audience. I couldn't tell if people were saying, "Oh, sure, I'll bet they are" or "That's awesome. We really are on top of things, but it's a well-kept secret." Either way, the eye rolling led me to believe that there was a glitch in their communication system.

Communication coordinators are in charge of ensuring that, as the old saying goes, the right hand knows what the left is doing. When done properly, this reduces the need to continually reinvent the wheel, and it also provides occasional opportunities to publicly celebrate the achievements gained.

Typically, communication coordinators are responsible for

- Assisting with the monitoring of RTI implementation in individual buildings and across the district.
- Developing and distributing brief monthly summary reports on building and district progress to both the faculty and community.
- Directing the development and maintenance of charts and graphs that illustrate how various programs and initiatives link to the RTI framework (see Figure 2.3).
- Establishing an RTI glossary to ensure that terms and acronyms don't create confusion or cause miscommunication.
- Writing and distributing newsletters to keep people focused on overall goals and the "big picture."

- Linking community resources to school problem-solving teams and professional development efforts.
- Helping parents identify interventions that might be helpful for their children.

Communication coordinators do not work in isolation. To help them accomplish their tasks, coordinators usually tap the knowledge, experience, and skills of school nurses, social workers, counselors, parent organization officers, booster club members, and fine and applied arts teachers.

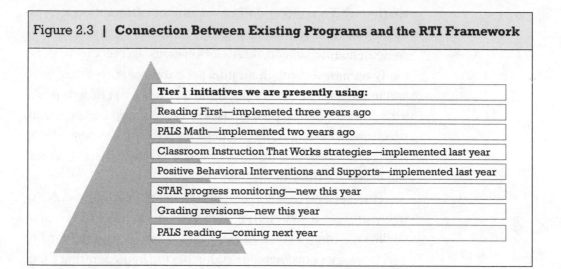

Figure 2.3 | **Connection Between Existing Programs and the RTI Framework**

Tier 1 initiatives we are presently using:

Reading First—implemeted three years ago

PALS Math—implemented two years ago

Classroom Instruction That Works strategies—implemented last year

Positive Behavioral Interventions and Supports—implemented last year

STAR progress monitoring—new this year

Grading revisions—new this year

PALS reading—coming next year

Technology coordinator

The difference between a district that integrates technology into its RTI plan and a district that does not is comparable to the difference between a transportation system that employs high-speed rail and one that relies on the horse and buggy. People still get to where they need to be in either case, but the latter is clearly less efficient and more time-consuming.

When the essential components of RTI are first introduced, the typical faculty response is a variation of "Yes, but . . .": "Yes, but who is going to do all the assessing and responding?" "Yes, but where are we going to find the time to do the work and recordkeeping?"

These are legitimate questions, and the use of technology is a critical part of the answer. Administering, scoring, and organizing assessments can consume hours of valuable instructional and planning time. However, most of the assessments required by an RTI process can be quickly administered, scored, and charted by a computer. Data from oral or observation assessments can also be transferred to a computer with a handheld device. Once organized, intervention ideas and records can be easily accessed through an internal database, providing easy and immediate access to potential solutions to student problems. Training can be provided via streaming video or webinars, which are accessed at the teacher's convenience. With the right mix of technology and training, time wasted on fruitless research can become a thing of the past.

These are just a few examples of how technology can effectively protect instructional time and energy. The list of possibilities is long, and each leadership team needs to identify a technology coordinator responsible for implementing time-saving ideas relevant to the needs and concerns of both teachers and students. Technology coordinators must regularly work closely with other members of the leadership team.

Technology coordinators collaborate with assessment coordinators to

- Implement computerized progress monitoring and other assessments.
- Create user-friendly charts and graphs that make data interpretation easy.

- Develop data storage and retrieval systems to make information more accessible and transferrable.
- Help teachers enter data into the assessment database.

Technology coordinators collaborate with pyramid coordinators to

- Establish and maintain an intervention database.
- Provide ongoing technology and intervention training for classroom application.

Technology coordinators collaborate with communication coordinators to

- Send regular progress reports to the community and faculty.
- Develop and maintain a resource Web site to help parents identify intervention ideas that might help their children.

Summary

When groups get discouraged, savvy leaders know when and how to move in and work alongside group members to identify problems, resources, and answers. Good leaders also recognize when groups have the skills to successfully solve problems on their own and only need encouragement and support from the sidelines. It is essential that everyone involved asks pertinent questions that keep work focused on achieving student results. Once leaders are adept at matching their individual leadership styles with the unique dynamics of problem-solving teams, the process invariably moves along much more smoothly.

Accurately matching leadership style with unique group dynamics allows for a much smoother and more fluid process.

I have heard it said, "We are perfectly aligned to get the results we are presently getting." If this is true, then a high achievement in reading and writing is caused by an effective alignment of language arts curriculum and instruction. By the same token, if behavioral issues and discipline occupy a considerable portion of instructional time, there must be a perfect alignment of factors that trigger behavior problems. This, therefore, should raise the question: "In our system, what needs realignment, and what is fine the way it is?"

In this chapter, we examined ways in which leadership teams can work together to reduce the number of fragmented initiatives and to increase options for solving problems. This kind of effort requires teamwork to effectively monitor and adjust plans. It also requires district and building teams to systematically analyze data, set clear goals, and establish support systems that build capacity among staff.

RTI is clearly not an easy road to quality education. People must move outside their comfort zones to make it successful. There will always be resistance to change and a reluctance to look at long-standing procedures and roles from a fresh perspective, but there are few who deny the urgency of helping students in need of support. Quality work can only be achieved through the dedication of committed teachers and administrators who keep student welfare as their primary focus.

In the next chapter, we will investigate efficient ways of collecting and analyzing data that enable teachers to judge the effectiveness of their interventions.

3

It's Not the Tool,
It's the Operator

When I was young, I remember getting frustrated because I couldn't make something as simple as a hammer work as well as my father could. When he had hammer in hand, nails never bent in half or veered sideways—they always went in straight and true. He made it look so easy.

I also remember my dad losing his temper when he couldn't find the tool he needed, usually because one of his six children had "borrowed" it to hold down one side of a blanket fort or for any number of other imaginative childhood uses. My father loved his tools and made sure that the ones he chose were quality. He always said that any job could be made easier if you had the right tool and knew how to use it properly.

The same can certainly be said of RTI. Quality tools are essential, but putting the right tools and the right people in place is only half the job. People need to know when to use a certain tool and when not to. Using a screwdriver to drive in a nail is possible but clearly not efficient.

In this chapter, we will discuss the variety of quality RTI assessment tools available and when to use them. It is likely that many of these assessments are already in place in your building or district. A few ideas, such as curriculum-based measurement (CBM), may be new to you. As you read this chapter, continue to think about where your district should adapt or replace older methods with more efficient ones. It might be painful at first, but discarding a few obsolete or inefficient plans and tools in favor of research-based, results-oriented ones is ultimately a good thing.

Let's listen in on the following conversation as Frank introduces RTI assessment tools to Eileen.

Frank: Eileen, don't forget our team meeting at 9:15.

Eileen: Darn. Why today? I'm buried under a mountain of work. The last thing I want to do is listen to people whine about kids who don't do their homework and parents who don't care enough to make them do it.

Frank: Actually, we have a serious agenda this time. Adrian is talking about a big revamp of the district assessments. The grapevine from the middle school says it's pretty impressive.

Eileen: Frank, let's face it, Adrian can sell ice cubes to polar bears. Unless she's planning to abandon all the useless testing we do, I'll be hard to impress.

Frank: Actually, it sounds like she's replacing much of the achievement testing with what she calls universal screening and progress monitoring. I guess we're talking about short, quick probes that only take a few minutes but are done regularly and scored right away.

Eileen: Sounds like we're shuffling the deck chairs on the *Titanic* again.

Frank: It could be, but at least we'll have the test results before they're too old to be useful.

The collection and use of assessment data is in serious need of reevaluation. Albert Einstein reportedly had a sign hanging in his office that read, "Not everything that counts can be counted, and not everything that can be counted counts." To make data collection count, you must actively use the information and not just record it. To make it count even more, you must use that information to fix the entire system and not just individuals.

The RTI framework uses three types of assessment tools to set goals and measure progress toward those goals as efficiently and thoroughly as possible.

1. **Universal screening** quickly identifies which students are at risk and which programs are working. It also gives a long-term look at student progress over multiple years.
2. **Diagnostic assessments** identify the root causes of problems.
3. **Progress monitoring** tracks the short-term rate of growth (weekly or biweekly).

Universal Screening

Many professions utilize screening methods to quickly identify problem situations. Doctors use screens such as general observations, body temperature, and blood pressure to determine which patients are healthy and which require a deeper diagnosis with possible treatment and monitoring. Auto mechanics check fluid levels to quickly determine which parts of a vehicle might require further attention. In the RTI process, universal screening activities help educators quickly identify which programs and students need further attention and more careful consideration.

The purpose of these screening activities is to predict possible problem academic and behavior areas and identify areas of strength. In order to achieve this goal, students should be screened three times a year in math, reading, writing, and behavior. Initial screening in the fall determines how many, and which, learners will require special attention with respect to their academic and behavioral skills. Teachers place these students on a "watch list" of potentially struggling learners. High schools often use results of achievement tests given at the end of 8th grade to identify incoming freshmen for their initial watch list and then verify the list with other screens. This will be further discussed in Chapter 4.

Screening results during the winter and spring call attention to learners who may have seemed on-level early in the year, but who lag behind as the material becomes more difficult. The district council then compares the fall, winter, and spring results to measure how well each building is progressing toward district goals. These data help identify which programs are draining teachers' time and energy without successfully closing student achievement gaps.

Some districts use high-stakes tests and achievement tests for universal screening; however, very few of these tests meet the criteria for a high-quality screening tool. The biggest drawback of this approach is the inability to validly administer achievement tests more than once a year. Quality universal screens are

- Aligned to the curriculum and assess age-appropriate skills.
- Easy to administer and require very little time (usually one to eight minutes).
- Repeatable within the same school year.
- Reliable and valid measures of student achievement.
- Sensitive enough to show small changes in achievement.

- Simple to score (they are often computer scored) and yield timely results.

HOW TO . . . *schedule universal screenings*

It is wise to schedule all three screening dates on the district calendar for the same weeks each year as nearly as possible. This allows teams to compare group results from year to year with greater reliability.

Curriculum-based measurement

The most reliable (and user-friendly) instrument for both universal screening and progress monitoring is curriculum-based measurement (CBM) because it meets all the criteria listed above. CBM not only facilitates the establishment of districtwide goals, but it also provides individual teachers with weekly feedback on improvement rates throughout the year.

Teachers sometimes have a hard time believing that such a simple tool can provide such worthwhile information. As the saying goes, "You don't have to drink the whole gallon of milk to see if it is sour"; so too is the thinking behind CBM probes. Probes are quick samplings of all major skill areas from the entire year's curriculum (e.g., in early reading, major curricular components are included in several one-minute probes; in math, students are given two and a half minutes to attempt 25 representative computation problems from material covered in the grade level).

Individual problems on CBM probes can change throughout the year, but each CBM must reflect the same concepts and remain at the same level of difficulty. Since the same skills and abilities are measured each time, an "apples to apples" comparison of global competence is therefore possible. As teachers chart student growth, they can easily see which students are steadily improving and making upward progress on the CBM graph throughout the year.

Since CBM measures the same skills and concepts all year, an "apples to apples" comparison is possible.

Research has demonstrated that CBM is more sensitive for detecting student growth than are most other assessment methods (VanDerHeyden, 2005). Studies in elementary schools show CBM to be a reliable and valid method of measuring student growth and achievement (Stecker, Fuchs, & Fuchs, 2005). Studies also show that CBM correlates highly with high-stakes and achievement tests (Good & Jefferson, 1998), and it is far less intrusive on instructional time since it is generally administered in less than eight minutes (Silberglitt, Burns, Madyun, & Lail, 2006).

You can create CBMs yourself or purchase programs developed by researchers (Hosp, Hosp, & Howell, 2007). Internet CBM resources include the following:

- Renaissance Learning, www.renlearn.com
- AIMSweb, www.aimsweb.com
- Dynamic Indicators of Basic Early Literacy Skills (DIBELS), http://dibels.uoregon.edu
- Edcheckup, www.edcheckup.com
- Intervention Central, www.interventioncentral.org
- System to Enhance Educational Performance (STEEP), www.isteep.com
- Yearly ProgressPro, www.mhdigitallearning.com

HOW TO . . . *select the best tool for you*

The National Center on Response to Intervention (www.rti4success.org) can help with your selection. This site contains a list of specific screening and monitoring tools reviewed by the center's technical review committee.

Diagnostic Assessments

Once a doctor has observed that blood pressure or body temperature is outside the expected range, he or she then gathers more specific information. The greater the abnormality of a patient's vitals, the more intensive the diagnostics become in order to identify root causes of the problem. The same is true in an educational setting once universal screening raises the initial "red flags."

Universal screening data help districts identify systemwide problems by identifying which learners are performing well and which are performing poorly. For example, if there is an area with less than 80 percent student proficiency, a diagnostic assessment is required to "dig deeper." You may develop hypotheses about what is causing the poor performance, but diagnostic data can more acutely validate or challenge these hypotheses. Here are a few issues to consider as possible poor performance culprits:

Diagnostic data "dig deeper" to validate or challenge hypotheses about what causes poor performance.

- Are both the core curriculum and the classroom management procedures research-based and followed with fidelity?
- Are research-based instructional and class management strategies used in every class on a daily basis?
- Are ample resources, time, and training provided to successfully implement high-yield strategies?
- Are all programs and services precisely coordinated with the core curriculum and class management plans, or are they operating in isolation?

At the building and classroom levels, there are several types of assessments teachers can use to diagnose problems. Most tests and quizzes teachers currently use on a daily basis can help them recognize student error patterns that can guide decisions about instruction and intervention. Unfortunately, these tools are not used diagnostically nearly enough. Examples of helpful daily diagnostic tools include

- Performing an error analysis of universal screening data.
- Analyzing samples of class work or project results.
- Using a "five reasons" analysis (described in Chapter 7) to uncover root causes for student or group problems.

- Analyzing course or grade-level assessment results and scoring them against a common rubric.
- Analyzing error patterns observed in CBM probes.

Diagnostic information allows teams to flexibly group learners as their individual needs change. These results also help to identify appropriate strategies for specific types of instruction or intervention. Consistent scoring guidelines used by all teachers are critical for maximum efficiency in diagnosing strengths and weaknesses. Teachers, of course, also need suitable training and time in their schedules to analyze work as a team.

Progress Monitoring

"Measure twice, cut once" is the adage for efficient carpentry work. In the RTI framework, the same wisdom prevails in order to avoid spending time on plans that don't work. A universal screening tool gives you an idea of which students need extra help or of which programs are weak. Diagnostic assessments tell you exactly what needs to be addressed by identifying causes of poor performance. Frequently measuring and charting growth (i.e., progress monitoring) verifies whether or not the correct strategies have been applied.

Progress monitoring probes are repeatedly administered to either individuals or groups. Keep in mind that they don't tell you exactly what causes student progress (or lack thereof)—that is the purpose of diagnostic assessments—but they do provide a quick and efficient method to see if you are on the right track. As mentioned previously, CBM is not only the best approach to universal screening, but also the most efficient technique to monitor progress.

Because CBM is highly sensitive to small gains, a teacher can see within weeks if a student is responding positively to the selected strategies. Instructional changes needed for maximum growth can therefore be made in a timely manner. Ideally, teachers don't waste time on strategies or programs that are not having the desired effects. A continuous cycle of "teach, check, and adjust" keeps the RTI process healthy.

Ultimately, quality progress monitoring tools must meet the same criteria as quality universal screening tools. They must be simple, be sensitive to small increments of growth, provide quick feedback, and provide specific information that leads to direct action. Appropriate tools vary according to grade level:

CBM allows teachers to see within weeks if a student is responding positively to the selected strategies.

- Kindergarten: letter recognition, letter sound fluency, number recognition
- Grade 1: nonsense word fluency, oral reading fluency, word identification, math computation
- Grades 2 and 3: oral reading fluency, math computation, math concepts and application fluency, writing and spelling fluency
- Grades 4–8: oral reading fluency, Maze reading, vocabulary/definition matching, writing fluency, spelling fluency, math computation, math concept/application
- Grades 9–12: Maze passages to check reading comprehension, vocabulary/definition matching probes, math computation, writing fluency probes

Progress monitoring with CBM

Standardization of CBM measurement, administration, and scoring is essential to achieving consistency among the tests. This consistency enables educators to reliably measure improvement rates for both individuals and groups over time. To ensure quality, both teachers and administrators must have adequate and appropriate training. Training procedures generally cover (1) how to guide the short practice exercises on CBM probes, (2) implementation of probes with precise timing, and (3) specific directions for administering and scoring CBM probes. Careful administration of CBM is critical since any

Standardized administration and scoring allow CBM results to reliably measure the rate of improvement over time.

deviation in delivery, scoring, and timing can render the scores invalid.

⚙ HOW TO . . . *begin setting up a progress monitoring system*

Consider the following questions as you begin the process of implementing a progress monitoring system. Answers will help guide the process in a beneficial and constructive direction.

- What district goals are we monitoring?
- What instruments will we use to monitor these goals?
- How often and by whom will this monitoring take place?
- What training will be needed?
- What support needs to come from the district level?
- Who will facilitate the process?
- How will progress be monitored and charted? How often and by whom?
- How will progress be analyzed and reported? How often, by whom, and to whom?

The amount of time it takes to administer a CBM probe is less than one class period per content area. The exact amount of time required depends upon several variables, including size of the school, number of trained staff assigned to the process, whether the probes are computer-based, and whether the probes are a group paper–pencil test or a one-on-one oral assessment.

⚙ HOW TO . . . *save time while progress monitoring*

- With eight assessors implementing individually administered three-minute probes, screening of a classroom of 24 students takes approximately 15 minutes.
- If the assessment is completed online, teachers can administer screens to an entire class at once without additional personnel. Many computer programs score CBM results automatically, thus adding very little to a teacher's overall workload.

With struggling students, start with material at the difficulty level that you expect them to master by the end of the school year. The material selected should be challenging but not so difficult that the student stumbles over every other word or problem. Students with IEPs may receive the allowable accommodations written on their IEPs, but teachers should not compare these scores to those derived without the same accommodations.

A rule suggested by Linda Fuchs (Fuchs & Fuchs, 2009) to guide this process in 1st–6th grade reading classrooms is: if the student reads fewer than 10 words correctly per minute, or if he or she reads 10–50 correct words per minute but is less than 85 percent correct, try a lower level. If the student reads more than 50 words per minute correctly, move to the next highest level where the student's fluency is 10–50 correct words per minute.

This same principle applies to math computations, concepts, and applications. If the student's average rate is fewer than 10 correct responses per time period allotted, the material may be too difficult. If the student averages more than 15 correct responses per time period, he or she may need to move to a higher level (Fuchs & Fuchs, 2009).

Each CBM probe has a unique scoring guideline, and just as administering CBMs must be standardized, scoring must also be uniform. There are several different types of scoring guidelines available.

Words identified *(grades K–1) Students are given 50 words randomly selected from a bank of 100 high-frequency words. They are then scored on the number of words read correctly in one minute.*

Oral reading fluency *(grades 1–12) Students orally read a selected passage for one minute. Errors include incorrect words, mispronounced words, substituted words, omitted words, transposed words, and a hesitation for five seconds that results in a need to have the word prompted. Scoring is calculated by the total number of words read minus the errors. Both the number of errors per minute and the words correctly read per minute can be* *charted. To establish an initial baseline score, three one-minute probes are given, and the median score is used as the baseline.*[1]

Math computation fluency *(grades 1–12) After students complete as many problems as possible in the allotted time, this probe is scored by counting the number of digits in the correct place rather than the number of correct answers. Tracking individual digits, rather than full answers, allows this CBM to be more sensitive to small growth changes.*

Math concepts and applications *(grades 2–12) Students respond to as many of the 18–30 math questions as they can in the time allotted for their grade level (generally 5–10 minutes). The questions are typically a sampling of math reasoning, measurement, probability, geometry, and estimation. Additionally, these questions require a minimum amount of computation. Scoring is done by counting the number of blanks correctly filled in. These could be one-word answers, multiple-choice items, short explanations, or estimates to solve problems (see www. rti4success.org for K–6 scoring guidelines).*

Writing fluency *(grades K–12) Students are provided with a sentence starter; they think about what they intend to write for one minute, and then they write for three minutes. This probe can be scored in three ways:*

- *Words written per three minutes—total words written minus incorrectly spelled words*
- *Letters written per minute—total number of letters written (controls for words of varying length)*
- *Number of correct sequences—total consecutive correct words (controls for grammar, spelling, capitalization, and punctuation). While this method is more time-consuming, this is the style that yields the most information.*[2]

Vocabulary match *(grades 8–12) Students are given 20 terms and 22 definitions randomly selected from a larger list of key vocabulary, and they must match the terms with the appropriate definitions.*

---

[1] See www.interventioncentral.org for detailed scoring tips in many areas; navigate to the manual located under "CBM Warehouse."
[2] See www.interventioncentral.org and www.rti4success.org.

This probe is particularly well suited to content-area classrooms such as science and social studies. Scores are calculated by the number of correct responses in five minutes.

Frequency of progress monitoring

As many teachers understand all too well, time given to testing is usually time lost for instruction. Therefore, achieving the right balance between testing and instruction is critical. For instance, you can monitor progress every three weeks if you use three probes when you assess.

However, herein lies the danger of not performing progress monitoring frequently enough. Due to the lack of timely feedback, a teacher can continue to implement an ineffective strategy for weeks without recognizing a pattern of nongrowth. Consequently, it is wise to let the frequency of progress monitoring depend upon the level of difficulty a student is experiencing. Your district should establish rules to guide this decision. Some questions to consider as you make these decisions are

> Frequency of progress monitoring should depend upon the level of difficulty a student is experiencing.

- What benchmark score will be used to identify students who are predicted to be successful using the core curriculum? Do these students need to be monitored more than three times a year?
- What benchmark score will identify students at slight risk? Do these students need to be monitored once a week? Every two weeks?
- What score will indicate students at a more serious risk? Is weekly monitoring enough for these students?
- Which students are already identified as experiencing a significant gap in their learning? How often should these students be monitored so teachers know when to change strategies?

Summary

In this chapter, we investigated the tools of the RTI assessment system. Without the frequent feedback of assessment data, teachers often find themselves putting effort into plans and instructional approaches that do not work. The tools described in this chapter help maintain focus and energy when they are used correctly.

A top-quality RTI data and analysis system does three things: (1) it clearly identifies areas of strength and concern with universal screening, (2) it identifies the root causes for areas of concern using diagnostic assessments, and (3) it helps track growth using progress monitoring tools. This assessment system enables teams to clearly see exactly what needs to happen next.

Remember that CBM assessments (as universal screening instruments or progress monitoring tools) do not diagnose the reasons for problems, but they do provide the simplest and most reliable methods to gather data on student growth patterns. CBMs quickly reveal whether a particular instructional approach or intervention plan is having the desired effect.

No matter which tools are selected, leadership teams, with the support of the assessment coordinator, need to ensure that proper training and fidelity monitoring are available to all staff. Only then can the assessment results provide reliable data for decision making, not just compliance.

Simply collecting and filing data is much like spitting into the wind—not much fun and certainly not effective. In the next chapter, we will examine the decision-making process using data that result from these assessment tools.

For more details and examples of CBM scoring, check the following sources:

- Center on Instruction, www.centeroninstruction.org
- Intervention Central, www.interventioncentral.org (navigate to the manual located under "CBM Warehouse")
- Espin, C. A., Shin, J., & Busch, T. W. (2005). Curriculum-based measurement in the content areas: Vocabulary-matching as an indicator of social studies learning. *Journal of Learning Disabilities, 38*(4), 353–363.
- Vanderbilt University Iris Center, http://iris.peabody. vanderbilt.edu/module_outlines/classroom_assessment_02.pdf
- National Center on Student Progress Monitoring, www. studentprogress.org

4

Using Universal Screen Results to Set Goals

Goals must be established at five levels to have maximum impact: district, building, grade, classroom, and student.

Many schools dabble in improvement efforts year after year only to find the same problems resurfacing. A major reason schools end up spinning their wheels in this way is the lack of a systemic plan. When buildings and teachers operate in isolation, they unfortunately resemble hamsters on wheels, running for all they're worth and not making any headway. For improvements to have maximum impact, coordinated goals must be pursued on five distinct levels. The district council sets systemwide goals, individual schools refine these goals into versions appropriate for the building and each grade level, and teachers then set classroom and individual student goals. In this chapter, we will look at specific examples of how to make systemwide decisions using focused assessment data.

Setting District Goals

One job of the district council is to establish goals that have a high impact on achievement. The council first studies data on learning environments and on patterns of academic achievement. It then identifies key areas for improvement and ranks these by priority of concern.

Examples of learning environment issues include the

- Number of attendance, mobility, and dropout problems.
- Number and types of behavior referrals and where these problems occur.
- Qualifications and attendance of teachers.
- Level of active administrator involvement in planning and monitoring improvement efforts.
- Level of collaboration among teachers in planning and implementing instruction.
- Efficient use of time in class or during meetings.

Examples of academic achievement issues include the

- Percentage of graduates who require remedial courses in college.
- Number of students in each grade who fail courses each year.
- Achievement scores of subgroups (e.g., special education, economically disadvantaged, English language learners, gifted).
- Reading, math, and writing achievement results from universal screening tools.
- Evidence that various programs close student achievement gaps.
- Number of research-based instructional practices used daily in classrooms.

Using diagnostic assessments to refine district goals

After reviewing environment and academic issues, the district council should select two or three critical concerns for the district team to study. The team then diagnoses the root causes of these problems. The following is an example of how this might play out.

After studying the data, the Ottawa district council notices that 41 percent of the freshman class has one or more *F*s in core subjects. The data also indicate that this is not unique to the current year's class. Although not nearly as severe, grades 4, 5, and 7 also have high numbers of failing grades on report cards. The council thus identifies the problem and a preliminary "plan of attack." *Problem 1: Too many failing grades. What is causing this? Ask the building teams to diagnose this problem and report back.*

The council also discovers that only 48 percent of district students across all grades are scoring at or above the benchmark proficiency level for writing. As the council analyzes the types of errors made on high-stakes tests, they recognize that writing is a primary contributor to poor performance. This weakness is corroborated by low scores from the universal writing screen performed in September. As a result, the council identifies another concrete problem. *Problem 2: Poor writing skills. Have each building analyze why this is so.*

This district chooses the DATA format for writing goals (Searle, 2007). The acronym DATA stands for

D—**D**ifferent interventions used by staff (i.e., new strategies and procedures)
A—new **A**chievement level expected from students
T—amount of **T**ime until the goal can be achieved
A—**A**ssessment evidence that indicates if the goal has been accomplished

Council members start writing a district DATA goal to guide the school improvement effort for the first year of a three-year commitment. They hypothesize that if writing scores improve, other test scores and grades will also improve.

D —

A — students will score at or above a proficient level for writing in all grades; failing grades will decrease

T — May of the following school year

A — 40 percent fewer Fs on report cards; 75 percent of students making adequate or better progress on CBM writing probes and the state assessment test; 22 percent increase in writing scores over a year and a half

This DATA goal is missing the *D* part of the goal—different approaches by staff. Each building then diagnoses its own writing program and related problems to identify specific causes of poor student writing achievement. The completed goal is written only after these causes are diagnosed and compiled by the building teams, which then complete the DATA goal to suit their unique situations.

Districts establish an overall goal, and individual buildings then decide what they need to do differently to help accomplish this goal.

Setting Building and Grade Goals

As staff members in the various buildings diagnose probable causes, they come up with two significant concerns: district guidelines for standardized grading are nonexistent, and there is no consistent districtwide plan for teaching the writing processes. As the teams learn more about how grades are calculated, they see how illogical it is. Students' grades do not necessarily reflect learning. For example, a paper that earns an *A* in one teacher's class may earn a *D* in another's. Many times, grades are radically influenced by student compliance to rules such as turning in homework on time or having a good attitude. Grades are sometimes changed simply because students choose to earn extra credit by means that have no correlation to learning. In one class, students even receive extra credit for bringing in a box of tissues and being in their seats when the bell rings. Although each of these procedures makes absolute sense to the individual teachers who use them, the lack of consistency results in unreliable grade values and the inability to use grades to draw conclusions about student achievement and progress.

After listening to the building teams' concerns, the district council responds. It establishes a team to recommend new grading guidelines for writing classes and another team to investigate research-based writing processes that will result in a coherent K–12 curriculum. To achieve the aggressive district goal, there is general agreement that all content areas need to be actively involved in the effort. This requires training and support at both the district and building levels.

To this end, all students are given three-minute writing probes three times a year. The students on the "watch list" are monitored once, and sometimes twice, a week. The district data team scores and charts the results for each class on a monthly basis, and the technology coordinator prepares visual reports for teachers that illustrate class growth since the previous probe.

Reports for individual grades and buildings help the district council and building leadership teams determine if the student improvement rate is on track to achieve the district goal. If growth is less than adequate, the building team first ensures that the Tier 1 writing curriculum is implemented with a high degree of fidelity. If all parts of the program are implemented as designed, then the focus can shift to diagnosing individual student problems and ways to supplement their core instruction with more intense Tier 2 or Tier 3 research-based interventions.

A middle school building team analyzes the situation in its particular school and completes its own DATA goal, written to correspond to the district goal:

> **D** — All teachers will select from the list of prescribed universal classroom interventions and implement progress

Reviewing data regularly at all levels keeps everyone focused on the district goal.

monitoring and mentoring programs focused on writing across the curriculum.

A — Failure rate at the middle school will drop in all core content areas; writing scores will improve.

T — June 5 of this school year.

A — Total Fs will decrease from 437 to fewer than 220; 76 percent of students will demonstrate growth close to or better than their CBM goal lines in writing.

The 4th grade teachers at one of the district's elementary schools analyze their school's nonfiction reading data and see that, as 3rd graders, 33 percent of their students performed poorly on the state test and 37 percent scored below average on the universal screening administered in September. Using this data, the teachers decide to place the lowest 40 percent of 4th grade students on the "watch list." The top 10 percent of these students receive individual student goals that are based on a "realistic" growth pattern.

Taking the district goal and their own circumstances into account, the 4th grade teachers construct the following DATA goal:

D — Teachers will implement at least four of the five new reading strategies selected by staff to address reading in the content areas.

A — 4th grade students will score at or above the proficient level in reading nonfiction text.

T — May 26 of this school year.

A — All students will meet their personal CBM norms for fluency and comprehension; 12 percent increase on the state achievement test.

Setting Classroom and Student Goals

Teachers can set realistic or ambitious growth rate goals based on national norms of students working at the 50th percentile. To see if students are growing at an appropriate rate to meet these goals, teachers create progress monitoring charts with goal lines that help guide decision making. Goal lines are established by drawing a line between a student's baseline score at the beginning of the school year and his or her projected score at the end of the year.

For example, if a group of 2nd grade students collectively scores at a rate of 30 correct words per minute during the sixth week of the school year, and the teacher projects an additional 60 words by the end of the school year, these students will close the learning gap and ultimately score at the expected rate of 90 words per minute. A visual goal line that charts their expected progress from 30 to 90 allows teachers to compare projected gains with actual student scores each time they are monitored for progress (see Figure 4.1). Continual charting helps teachers determine whether classroom strategies are working.

To design your own chart, begin by labeling the student's name, grade level, and subject. The particular skill being measured should be aligned along the vertical axis (the range should incorporate the lowest and highest expected scores for this particular probe). For example, the vertical axis could represent a range of words read correctly per minute or a range of minutes spent consecutively focused on task. The number of instructional weeks in the school year (either actual dates or numbered weeks), from the week of the initial probe to the end of the school year, should be aligned along the horizontal axis.[1]

---

[1] There is a CBM growth calculator and graphing program developed by Gwen Sweeny and Joseph Jenkins available from the University of Washington that simplifies the graphing of CBM progress. It can be downloaded from www.fluentreader.org.

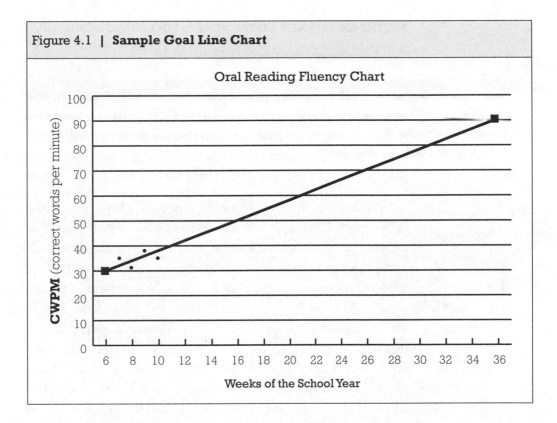

Figure 4.1 | Sample Goal Line Chart

Oral Reading Fluency Chart

Ronald's 4th grade teacher, Mrs. Tackett, uses a realistic improvement rate of .7 words per week to calculate Ronald's growth for the year. There are 30 weeks of instruction left in the year, so Mrs. Tackett multiplies .7 words per week by 30 remaining weeks and predicts that Ronald will increase his fluency 21 words per minute by the end of the year. Ronald already reads at 99 words per minute, so Mrs. Tackett adds this to his projected improvement rate and predicts a year-end total fluency rate of 120 words per minute. This prediction indicates that Ronald will be reading slightly below the expected rate for his grade level (130 words per minute) by the end of the year. In this scenario, Ronald's initial score on the graph is 99, his projected final

Individual goals are set using realistic norms for students with small gaps and aggressive norms for students with large gaps.

score is 120, and Mrs. Tackett draws a line connecting these two scores to illustrate his goal line.

HOW TO . . . *calculate goals*

Multiply the expected rate of weekly improvement by the number of weeks left in the school year. This provides the predicted increase for the year, assuming that the student receives effective interventions. Add this score to the student's existing achievement level.

While realistic goals work for students who score at and above grade-level expectations, students who score below these expectations will never close the learning gap without accelerating their growth beyond the normal rate. Lower-achieving students require goals calculated with ambitious rates to reduce significant gaps. This approach, however, flies in the face of antiquated school practices that tend to "water down" and slow down appropriate instructional pacing for underperforming students. Of course, it is counterproductive to set ambitious goals if ambitious instructional plans, such as Tier 2 and Tier 3 interventions, are not in place to support the achievement of those goals.[2]

Ambitious goals are only achievable if ambitious instructional plans are in place.

Norm tables vary among researchers and publishers because different materials are used in their respective studies. Figures 4.2 and 4.3 represent average norm values for reading and math growth among K–12 students. I use these guidelines as a rule of thumb for setting both realistic goals (50th percentile expected rate of improvement) and ambitious goals for individual students or groups of students.

---

[2] Many different norm tables are available to help guide the process of setting student goals. One is the Hasbrouck-Tindal table of national oral reading fluency norms for grades 1–8. This is available online at www.readnaturally.com/howto/whoneeds.htm. Alternatively, look in the CBM presentation materials available at www.studentprogress.org.

A variation of expected grade-level norms is possible since rates are based on the difficulty of administered probes. If your district does not use a program with preestablished norms, you may need to determine norms unique to your situation. To determine improvement goals for subgroups or entire classes, the formula is the same as that used for individual students (i.e., multiply the expected weekly rate of improvement by the number of instruction weeks remaining), but use the class average from the universal screening as the baseline.[3]

Grade Level	Realistic Rate of Weekly Improvement	Expected Grade-Level Norm	Ambitious Rate of Weekly Improvement
Figure 4.2 | Reading Growth Norm Table			
	Letter–Sound Correspondence (letters correct)		
K	1		1.5
	Oral Reading Fluency (words correct per minute)		
1	2	60	3
2	1.5	90	2
3	1	105	1.5
4–5	.7	130	1
6–12	.5	150	.8
	Maze Probe (correct replacements per 2.5-minute probe)		
3	.4	15–20	.6
4	.4	20–24	.6
5	.4	24–28	.6
6–12	.4	20–30	.6

[3] Monitor Web sites such as www.progressmonitoring.org, www.centeroninstruction. org, and www.studentprogress.org for updates as new research becomes available.

Grade Level	Realistic Rate of Weekly Improvement	Expected Grade-Level Norm	Ambitious Rate of Weekly Improvement
Figure 4.3 | Math Growth Norm Table			
Grade Level	Realistic Rate of Weekly Improvement	Expected Grade-Level Norm	Ambitious Rate of Weekly Improvement
Computation Fluency (digits correct*)			
1–3	.3	20–50	.45
4–8	.6	30–35	1
Concepts and Applications (blanks filled in correctly*)			
1–3	.4	20	.6
4–8	.7	15–25	1

* = data based on two-minute probes in grades 1–3 and five-minute probes in grades 4–8

Making Decisions Along the Way

Research shows that establishing clear goals and providing specific feedback directly leads to enhanced student achievement, improved teacher decision making, and greater student motivation (Fuchs, 1991). Progress monitoring helps maintain clear and specific feedback used to make data-driven instructional decisions.

When a doctor orders an MRI to identify the cause of a medical problem, the data are helpful but do nothing to directly cure the patient. Likewise, collecting data in an educational setting is valuable but not worth the time and effort if the data are not used to "find the cure." Only when assessment data are considered to be an instructional decision-making tool can the benefits of progress monitoring be fully realized.

Deciding how to proceed

RTI assessment is not about "one-shot" tests. Rather, it is about charting data points that illustrate a trend. Rules must therefore be established to help educators make consistent decisions as they use this information. For example, six to eight data points could be collected and graphed to show a pattern of growth. The graphs can then be used to make one of three

RTI assessment is not about "one-shot" tests. Rather, it is about charting data points that illustrate a trend and then using that information to make instructional decisions.

instructional decisions: continue with an approach or intervention that seems to be working, raise the goal in response to elevated student achievement, or abandon the intervention that is not working and try something new.

According to the Four-Point Rule (Figure 4.4), if the four most recent consecutive data points are below the goal line, a change in intervention should be considered. Do not change the goal; change the plan to reach the goal. If the four previous data points are above the goal line, consider resetting the goal to a more challenging level. Finally, if the data points hover very close to the goal line, the intervention is suitable and should continue as planned.

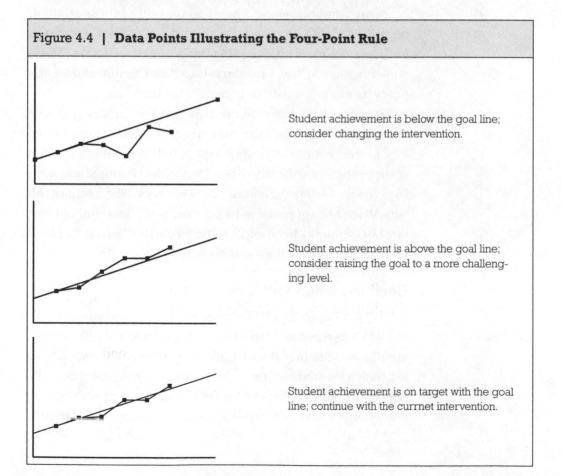

Figure 4.4 | Data Points Illustrating the Four-Point Rule

Student achievement is below the goal line; consider changing the intervention.

Student achievement is above the goal line; consider raising the goal to a more challenging level.

Student achievement is on target with the goal line; continue with the currnet intervention.

Deciding who needs additional support

Districts generally identify two benchmark scores that help make decisions about which students should be closely monitored. The first benchmark (or "cut score") usually encompasses all students whose scores raise even the slightest level of concern. Districts have the freedom and flexibility to set their respective cut scores as low or as high as necessary to reflect the number of students performing below expected levels.

For example, a certain district determines that 40 percent is its primary cut score. In other words, the lowest-performing 40 percent of students are in need of some level of intervention assistance. A teacher then analyzes her class universal screening scores and places the lowest 40 percent of these students on the watch list. In response, she sets an improvement goal for the entire class and for individuals on the watch list. These students receive Tier 1 research-based instruction and weekly progress monitoring in the general education class.

Students who score below a second benchmark (perhaps the lowest 16 percent of the class) receive extra monitoring and Tier 1 interventions. As a supplement to this instruction, many of these students may also need Tier 2 interventions, and a few (5 percent or so) may require Tier 3 services. The intent of this "double-dose" approach is to accelerate the learning of these targeted students in an effort to begin closing the gap between their actual achievement and expected goals.

Deciding when and how to change

My mother always told me not to be surprised when people balk at change because "the only people who actually like change are babies with dirty diapers, and even they don't always think it's such a great idea." Receptiveness to change often has to do with convenient timing and the level of discomfort with current conditions. A certain level of pushback is a normal and natural reaction to a shift away from one's comfort zone, and it should be an anticipated part of the process. It is therefore important to be sympathetic to the concerns and doubts of everyone involved if progress is to be made. A common statement of resistance is "I don't have time to do this." Busy professionals—administrators and teachers—often (and understandably) resist activity that they view as meaningless busywork assigned by others.

Explaining how screening and monitoring is implemented is not enough to ease concerns. Administrators need to focus on the fact that everyone's objective is to achieve maximum impact for the time, money, and energy devoted to each day. We all want to reduce discipline problems and increase the number of students in honors classes. We would rather prevent student failure than spend hours repairing the damage after the fact. We know we need information at people's fingertips to help them respond to student difficulties quickly. RTI done well helps all of us accomplish these objectives and more.

Once educators are convinced that screening and monitoring are commonsense approaches to perennial problems, buy-in comes much more easily. When they believe in a particular approach, staff will not only support it but typically focus on and dedicate time to it. However, when the rationale behind making a change is vague or questionable, people tend to challenge the process considerably.

> Real buy-in comes when RTI is demonstrably shown to help people accomplish the most important parts of their job more efficiently.

Forcing RTI assessment procedures into an overflowing curriculum is a high-risk way to start the process and implement change. It is vital that sufficient time is built into teachers' schedules for them to analyze and plan together. Obviously, finding this time, or deciding how to create it, can be fairly tricky. Two major administrative decisions help facilitate this process: reduce and replace current underproductive practices, and train staff to work in teams.

Data from universal screening, diagnostic analysis, and progress monitoring supply clues as to which programs, tests, and procedures are due for an upgrade or wholesale replacement.

There is a nearly universal agreement that overflowing schedules need to be trimmed. Unfortunately, precisely what to discard or reduce is rarely straightforward. However, RTI assessment results can effectively be used as a "measuring stick" to guide these decisions. Data from universal screenings, diagnostic analyses, and progress-monitoring tools supply clues as to which programs, tests, and procedures are due for an upgrade or wholesale replacement. Once the (sometimes contentious) deliberations over what needs to go are complete, replacing rather than adding assessment components will make sense and relieve stress.

Even the most enthusiastic teachers cannot meet the demands of a full RTI process by themselves. Cooperation and teamwork are two essential hallmarks of a successful RTI program. Cohesive teams, rather than individual teachers, must analyze and respond to data to make the system work most effectively. It is critical that consistent blocks of time are scheduled and maintained for all teachers so that teams can effectively analyze data and plan together. Just as important is ongoing professional development that teaches and fine-tunes efficient collaboration skills.

Deciding how to focus RTI efforts

Even if you design a regular and predictable schedule of meeting times, there is no guarantee that teams will maximize this time and make the meetings beneficial. Groups do not automatically become efficient teams with high-level data analysis discussions just because they have common planning time. Definite structure and guidelines for leading efficient meetings are just as important as the time itself. Teams need timed agendas and regular feedback on how well they stick to the agenda and the agreed-upon protocols. Respecting each others' time—by not wasting it on small talk and off-task discussions—is critical to a happy and productive environment.

HOW TO . . . *find extra team time*

1. In schools where teachers arrive 20 or more minutes before the student day begins, combine before-school time with homeroom and first period to provide teams with more than an hour to meet. On days when their teams meet, teachers will need someone to cover homeroom activities so the meetings are not interrupted. This same technique can be used at the end of the school day for another team. In this way, 10 teams can be scheduled each week. I have seen this successfully employed in both elementary and secondary schools.

2. Plan a quality monthly assembly for students. One-third of the faculty attends the assembly and helps supervise students, while the remaining two-thirds meet with their respective teams during this time.

3. Consider partner teaching and "big buddy" programs. When I taught in a K–8 school, 2nd and 8th grade teachers were paired with partner teachers in the other grade. Once a month, 2nd grade classes spent a period with their 8th grade partner classes for "big buddy" time. This not only provided time for 2nd grade teachers to meet, but it also created a unique learning environment for the students. Buddies discussed an assigned topic (which matched what each class was currently studying) and then discussed a film clip together. At another point in the month, the process was reversed and the 8th grade students visited the 2nd grade classrooms. Almost all students eagerly looked forward to their "buddy time," and it was a perfect way to gain an extra period of planning time for each grade. An additional benefit of this plan is that the once-a-month meeting doesn't detract at all from student learning. Secondary schools could easily adapt this idea and use it to integrate two content areas.

4. Provide individual schools with a budget for substitute teachers who move as a team throughout the building, taking classes for departments or grade levels that need to meet for a specific purpose.

5. Transform faculty meetings (once a venue for announcements and housekeeping chores) into data analysis or intervention development sessions.

One way to judge team productiveness is to calculate the percentage of meeting time used to discuss instruction versus administrivia. A good rule of thumb teams can follow is that 80 percent of their meeting time should be spent using data to

1. Plan what to teach.
2. Share strategies and resources for enhancing lessons.
3. Identify students who are still struggling.

4. Develop an instructional plan that targets struggling learners.
5. Decide how to accommodate students in need of lesson enrichment and extension.

The remaining 20 percent of team meeting time should be used for noninstructional topics such as these:

*   Student discipline
*   Parent conferences
*   Event planning (e.g., assemblies, field trips)
*   General housekeeping

If organization and training are not done well, teachers will inevitably resist any change to a revamped assessment process. Assessment coordinators can help make the transition simpler by helping principals and teacher leaders

*   Design and implement assessment overview meetings.
*   Decide which grade levels and content areas to focus on first.
*   Develop or purchase assessment materials in a timely manner.
*   Train teachers and data team members to administer the screening tool.
*   Create a timeline for collecting, scoring, and charting screening results.
*   Compile data in a visual display and distribute it to teachers before the analysis meeting.
*   Facilitate meetings shortly after each universal screening to analyze results and set goals.

Summary

When important decisions aren't based on data, data collection is usually seen as unnecessary and frustrating busywork. If data are gathered but not compared to a specific goal, no one thinks to ask, "Are we on target?" If asked, it can only be answered in the vaguest of terms, and appropriate action is rarely, if ever, taken.

When student data are not specific enough or not adequately graphed, teachers tend to lose focus on the goal and remark, "Well, I taught it. They just didn't learn it." When this happens, the focus on results has been lost.

Quality data analysis guides team discussions and leads to substantial decisions for improvement. Such research- and evidence-based decisions ultimately result in conversations becoming more honest, team members trying harder when it becomes obvious that their work is paying off, and groups feeling a sense of accomplishment. Problems also get solved faster and workloads become lighter when team members realize that work can be done more efficiently, thanks to reliable partners and information.

In the next chapter, we will address the question "So now I know what the problems are, according to the data. What are the solutions?"

5

The Tiered Pyramid
of Interventions

Marcus Long enters the pool area ready to take on his new crop of 4th grade swimmers from Mills Elementary School. He smiles as he checks his roster and watches the excitement and harmless horseplay happening in the pool. Most of the kids look like they have had lots of informal experience in the water. He notices one student doing laps with speed and skill. Marcus checks his notes. This is obviously Michael who is learning to swim competitively.

Marcus notices one child approaching the pool in a wheelchair. This must be Tony. Tony's aide lifts him into the water where he seems happy and comfortable. One student who doesn't seem so comfortable is perched on the side of the pool shivering, and she's not even wet. This reluctant participant must be Sonya. She has never been in a pool and obviously doesn't even like being close to one now.

As Marcus begins the first class, he explains that the goal is for everyone to swim across the pool and back by the end of the six-week session. Marcus begins class with some simple screening activities to see who already has basic skills and who will require extra help. Obviously, the group goal will not be suitable for everyone. Michael surpassed the benchmark long ago, so Marcus will help Michael set an individual goal that is more appropriate. It is tempting to lower the goal for Sonya and Tony. Sonya's extreme fear of water keeps her from venturing beyond the steps, but Marcus knows that it is wiser to find new strategies for Sonya and keep the goal where it is. He will allow Sonya to start with a "floatie" and play some games to boost her confidence. Similarly, Marcus will work with Tony and, despite Tony's disability, help him accomplish the goal with the assistance of swim fins. Marcus also plans to give advice and guidance to Sonya's and Tony's parents so they can help their children between lessons.

The Importance of the Pyramid

Like Marcus, teachers who use an RTI approach assess their students' strengths and weaknesses. They set group and individual goals that are reasonable but rigorous. They determine which instructional methods and supplemental supports will achieve the desired results without lowering goals, if possible. Teachers routinely collect data to keep themselves and their students continually aware of the progress and development that result from the strategies employed. If progress is not on target, the teacher selects a different evidence-based approach to get back on track and prevent educational "drowning."

In the past, teachers and problem-solving teams often missed the boat when it came to selecting interventions and instructional strategies. I routinely hear teachers say, "I go to meetings only to find that the problem-solving team's suggestions are no better than what I'm doing—have Mom sign his agenda book, shorten the assignments, read the test to her   ." Teachers want a variety of powerful interventions, but they often have a hard time finding them.

Pyramid coordinators, then, facilitate the development of a multitiered pyramid of interventions. The most common pyramid model consists of three tiers of increasingly intense interventions. For effective day-to-day implementation, teachers need a database of research-based ideas, along with a list of resource people who can explain and model these strategies. This pyramid is a bear to put together if tackled by only a few people. However, when an entire staff is mobilized to contribute to the process and identify teacher leaders who can successfully model and teach the new strategies, it can create a healthy sense of ownership and solidarity.

Organizing a pyramid of interventions and establishing an RTI plan can be a delicate process. Take, for instance, the example of Avon Lake, a small suburban district in northern Ohio. District teachers started by creating a list of concerns that came up yearly, including poor comprehension, inattention, poor writing fluency, and lack of follow-through, among many others. Each teacher chose to work on just one topic for the year, such as "bullying" or "remembering basic math facts." They agreed to find nine strategies that addressed their respective topic and represented a range of intensities, from "easy to implement in a large group" to "so intense it cannot be accomplished with more than three students at a time." The teachers had the will, skill, and enthusiasm to complete the task, but finding time was frustrating. Adding this task to already busy schedules began to feel like the proverbial straw that broke the camel's back.

The following month, the teachers came together and regrouped, both literally and figuratively. They decided that the task would be more manageable if grade-level teachers worked together. Therefore, each grade identified one academic problem and one behavioral problem that were ongoing sources of

Teachers need a database of research-based ideas, along with a list of resource people who can explain and model strategies.

frustration. As a team, they worked together to find strategies that addressed these issues. This created a sense of urgency since the information had relevance to their classrooms, and it was not just for a database. In addition, deciding to use the faculty meetings for this work solved the dilemma of time. In the end, the teachers found it surprisingly easy to regain momentum once time and the opportunity to pool efforts were made available.

Unleashing the unique creative energies of individual staff members is the best method to implement and provide RTI support. Building resource teams that can immediately share, model, and refine intervention ideas is much more efficient than depending upon experts who might be scattered around the state or country. This in-house group of mentors is called the "expert pool."

The expert pool promotes a culture of willingness to learn from one another—a hallmark of cohesive groups with solid leadership. Teachers in healthy collaborative environments typically celebrate each other's successes without jealousy. Minor setbacks simply create more determination among teams to work together, and student data are viewed as a road to instructional improvement instead of criticism and unhealthy competition. Committee-designed databases lack many of these benefits as groups tend to reject initiatives in which they have no creative investment.

Designing the Tiers

Designing a multitiered intervention model requires a realignment of general, gifted, remedial, and special education services. Since struggling students should receive at least part of their supplemental support in general education classrooms, special education teachers and other support services need to shift and share some of their roles and responsibilities.

Designing a multitiered intervention model requires a realignment of traditional roles and resources.

Resources also need to be realigned. A mental and physical inventory helps determine which strategies and programs work in the new model, where instructional gaps exist that require new programs, and which programs are inefficient and should be dropped. This requires willingness to change and the ability to rethink schedules, materials, locations, programs, grouping patterns, and other long-standing practices. The expert pool, under the guidance of the pyramid coordinator (as discussed in Chapter 2), plans this cooperative effort.

Tier 1 focuses on implementing quality research-based core instruction. A good Tier 1 plan includes such things as an aligned curriculum, differentiated instruction, formative assessment, specific and timely corrective feedback, a consistent positive behavior plan, and other strategies and programs proven through a rigorous research design to have a positive effect on student growth. These initiatives are designed to prevent academic and behavioral problems. If more than 16 percent of the students share a common problem, such as substandard writing skills or poor study habits, it is generally an indicator of a larger issue that needs to be addressed in the overall curriculum, instruction, or environment.

Tier 2 strategies suit smaller groups of students with homogeneous needs. It provides a double dose of instruction for students who missed key concepts and skills in the larger group setting. The hallmark of quality instruction at Tier 2 is fast-paced, high-interest instruction and regular corrective feedback. Teachers can often adjust approaches that work at this level to all three tiers. For example, peer tutoring can be used in Tier 1 with all students as pairs of classmates practice together while the teacher monitors progress and gives feedback. At Tier 2, limiting the group size to no more than six students enables the teacher to monitor them more closely and give more corrective feedback.

Tier 1 is research-based classroom instruction for all students. Tier 2 is supplemental support to Tier 1, and Tier 3 is the most intense level of instruction and support.

Tier 3 strategies involve modeling, direct instruction, paired practice, and individual practice. This level requires specialized training and often uses intensive programs. Therapists, ESL teachers, and special education teachers often design Tier 3. At this level, if only two students practice together, and the amount of time allocated is sufficient, the teacher can provide more frequent and focused modeling as well as more immediate corrective feedback.

It is extremely helpful if the pyramid includes lists of quick and easy interventions that parents can use with their children at home. This enables parent involvement to go beyond verbal support of classroom instruction. It goes further than homework help—which often, in and of itself, creates frustration within the family. The parent intervention database is a list of family-friendly strategies that target specific skills and promote true partnerships for problem solving. Further details for establishing these partnerships will be explained in Chapter 7.

HOW TO . . . *creatively initiate parent involvement*

Send home demonstration DVDs (or arrange for the videos to be available online) of specific strategies that parents can use with their children. If their child is featured in the video, you can bet that parents will make time to watch it.

You will find a variety of opinions among experts as to how the tiers should be defined, how long interventions should last each day, and how long support at each tier should last. In this book, I merge research from Vanderbilt University, The Florida Center for Reading Research, the University of Minnesota, and details from my own work with schools. RTI legislation is flexible enough to allow different approaches and adjustments to suit individual district needs. The bottom line is "Does your data show that your model works for your students?" If the answer is *yes*, then you must be doing something right. If the student growth pattern is weak, or if students are negatively affected by pressure exerted on them to achieve results, it is time to try something new.

Research-based strategies do not have to be elaborate, but it is critical that they are specific. A good intervention database spells out the processes so clearly that a teacher can easily replicate the intervention with fidelity. Each entry should identify the

- Skills addressed.
- Targeted grade levels.
- Materials needed for implementation.
- Recommended group size.
- Recommended session length.
- Frequency and duration required.
- Steps and tasks necessary for implementation.
- Plan for measuring and monitoring effectiveness.
- Source of the research-based idea.

Providing space for comments and tips allows teachers to make suggestions to future users who implement a particular strategy. Figure 5.1 shows a sample entry for the intervention database.

Tier 1 Instruction

If Tier 1 general education instruction is not adequate to support 80–90 percent of the students, there are three common causes the district council should investigate: weaknesses in core programs and procedures, a lack of fidelity of implementation, and weak alignment within the curriculum.

For example, if math scores are weak, the first question the council should ask is "Is our adopted math program research-based?" The term *research-based* refers to programs and interventions that have been reported in scientific, peer-reviewed journals as being effective with most students most of the time. Existing instructional tools and textbooks often do a poor job

> Research-based strategies do not have to be elaborate, but it is critical that they are specific.

| Figure 5.1 | **Pyramid Card, Sample 1** |

Teacher: Sara McDowell

Appropriate for Grade Levels: K–10

Date: December 2010

Intervention: Teaching Math Facts. This intervention is designed to build math fact fluency and increase accuracy. It can be used for addition, subtraction, multiplication, or division facts. It can be used at any tier.

Materials: timer; math flashcards with answers on the back (specifically selected for each student); math worksheet; progress charts

Frequency and Duration: eight minutes daily for at least six weeks, or until student meets grade-level fluency level

Instructional Steps (conduct these steps every day):
1. PEER PRACTICE: Math partners get out their personal set of flashcards. Tell students that you will let them practice with a partner for two minutes so they can try to beat their math scores from yesterday. Set the timer for two minutes and tell students, "Begin practicing with one set of cards." At the end of two minutes, say, "Stop. Now use the other set of flashcards." Set the timer for two minutes and prompt students to start and stop at the appropriate times.

2. TIMED PRACTICE: Pass out worksheets with approximately 25 problems. Tell the students to keep the papers face-down and write their name on the back of the paper. Set the timer for two minutes and say, "When I say 'go,' do as many problems as you can in two minutes." At the end of two minutes, have students exchange papers. Go through the problems on an overhead projector or pass out an answer key. Tell students to mark "C" for correct answers and circle incorrect answers.

3. ERROR CORRECTION: Tell students, "Give the papers back to their owners. If you have any errors, write the correct answer under the circled, incorrect answer. Then pull out the flashcards that match the problems you missed so you can study those before the math probe tomorrow." Have students mark their scores on their personal math progress charts.

4. REWARD/MOTIVATION: Announce the class average from yesterday and celebrate when the class beats this average score. Discuss what it will take from every student to move the score up again tomorrow.

Progress Monitoring: Correct a timed paper every Friday, and record that score on the official growth chart.

Research Basis: Robert Marzano's work on quality practice with charting (Marzano, R. J., Pickering, D. P., & Pollock, J. E. [2001]. *Classroom instruction that works: Research-based strategies for increasing student achievement*. Alexandria, VA: ASCD.)

Teacher Comments:

of adhering to important instructional principles for learning in mathematics (U.S. Department of Education, 2008). To identify specific research that supports the programs you are presently (or considering) using, go to the What Works Clearinghouse Web site (http://ies.ed.gov/ncee/wwc).

If poor results are not the result of inadequate programs, the next question councils should ask is "How well is our program being implemented?" It is not uncommon to adopt research-based math materials, only to find that some teachers skip the manipulatives and games and go straight to the worksheets. This is often contrary to the original design and intent of the materials, especially for "watch list" students. To prevent poor implementation, district and building teams need to establish a written plan for monitoring how programs and services are delivered. This plan should specify who will monitor the delivery, what practices will be used, and how often monitoring will be performed. The objective is to identify problem areas proactively, before damage is done.

The third source of Tier 1 dysfunction is the lack of horizontal alignment within a grade or course and vertical alignment between grades. The following example illustrates how a lack of alignment can have a domino effect on student achievement.

Several years ago, I observed an extremely talented kindergarten teacher who consistently helped children fall in love with story writing. By March, she typically had students happily writing stories that were pages long (kindergarten pages, but pages nonetheless). This happened year after year, yet the kindergarten teacher in the next room believed that asking young children to write stories was developmentally inappropriate. By March of each year, her students could not write a single sentence.

Fast-forward a year, and consider the 1st grade teachers whose incoming students came from both of these kindergarten classes. To compound matters, the two 1st grade teachers

> To prevent poor implementation, district and building teams need to establish a written plan for monitoring how programs and services are delivered.

were almost as far apart on writing expectations as were the kindergarten teachers. Are you starting to see what a complicated situation the 2nd grade teachers inherit? They will have an inordinately large group of "at-risk" writers, not because of their students' inability to learn, but because of the uneven expectations of the teachers.

When teachers develop common assessments with common rubrics and agreements for evaluation, coherent expectations eventually fall into line. Acceptable instruction and performance must be consistent at each grade level in order to recognize inadequate instruction. Only when Tier 1 instruction is safely ruled out as a cause of poor student performance can Tier 2 and Tier 3 interventions appropriately be considered.

A strong preK–12 vertical alignment is the infrastructure that enables teams to organize successful and efficient delivery of tiered interventions, programs, and services within the RTI framework. Templates for planning assessments and unit designs often help teams coordinate this work of vertical alignment.[1]

In Tier 1, students on the watch list are monitored weekly for progress, and they receive extra small-group assistance within the general education classroom. This typically lasts six to eight weeks. Students who show significant progress during this time may no longer require extra classroom help but still need monitoring to ensure that new skills are stable.

Whenever Tier 1 data illustrate a lack of growth (i.e., the student has four consecutive data points below the goal line), team members monitoring the RTI process must ask the following questions:

> Uneven expectations of teachers cause poor alignment in the curriculum.

---

[1] One such template can be downloaded from my Web site (www.margaretsearle. com). Also available is a resource book that shows ways to use this template and ways for specialists and general education teachers to work together (Searle, 2004). Ideas in this book are closely correlated with the work of Grant Wiggins, Jay McTighe, and Carol Ann Tomlinson.

- Is the teacher instructing and assessing with fidelity?
- Is the student using appropriate materials?
- Is the student getting a sufficient amount of classroom intervention per week?
- Should the teacher adjust or change the classroom interventions?

If the answer to any of the first three questions is *no*, then the pyramid coordinator (or another expert resource person) assists the teacher by modeling or consulting until the problem is identified and resolved.

HOW TO . . . *teach and assess with fidelity*

Implementing intervention strategies with fidelity is like taking an antibiotic. Once you start feeling better, you are tempted to stop taking the medication, or at least be less vigilant about how often you take it. Unfortunately, this laissez-faire attitude could find you right back in the sick bed. Implementing an intervention in a random way wastes time and energy and doesn't cure a thing. It is critical that teachers receive adequate training and feedback to avoid creating learning casualties.

One way that many schools address the need to provide feedback and embedded training is through the use of a walkthrough process. This process involves assembling three or four teachers and administrators charged with the responsibility to walk through several classrooms with the purpose of describing quality ways that teachers implement certain strategies. After the walkthrough, the team creates an overall report listing observed team strengths and identifying alternate implementation strategies. The next week, a new group is given the opportunity to observe and report on the same or a different strategy. Even though the walkthrough report to the team does not list teachers by name, the process of observing and being observed keeps everyone's skills sharp.

If the answer to the first three questions is *yes*, then the conditions for growth are in place. If the students still are not responding to the approach, the teacher should then select and employ a different intervention of the same intensity. At this point, the teacher might also recommend that Tier 2 interventions be considered as an additional option for certain students. A problem-solving team or coach will help diagnose the root cause of the problem and assist in deciding upon the next steps.

Tier 2 Support

The goal of Tier 2 supports is to close the achievement gap as quickly as possible. Students who do not make adequate progress in Tier 1 receive more intensive Tier 2 small-group services either within or outside the general education classroom. Tier 2 interventions include programs, strategies, and procedures that provide a "double dose" of support to accelerate learning.

Tier 2 often lasts from six to nine weeks and provides around 50 to 100 minutes of additional instruction per week on specifically targeted skills. These services are always "in addition to" and never "instead of" Tier 1 instruction. Students are encouraged to immediately apply skills learned in Tier 2 in the general education classroom.

The following conversation addresses common concerns teachers have about Tier 2 delivery. The suggestions are a composite of options used by schools with which I have worked.

> Tier 2 adds supplemental small-group instruction to Tier 1 to close the achievement gap as quickly as possible.

Kyle: I understand that Tier 2 needs to be a double dose of instruction and practice, but just where are we supposed to find this extra time?

Sandra: I don't know, but I'm sure glad they're not taking kids out of core classes and fine arts to get it. My students resented that last year, and so did I.

Kyle: Well, something has to give. What do other schools do to find intervention time?

Sandra: Riverside started before- and after-school tutoring groups. They alternate days between math and language arts. Kids sign up for six-week sessions and attend either two or all four days of the morning or afternoon sessions.

Kyle: The kids we really need to work with won't come to before- or after-school gigs.

Sandra: Northwestern High School schedules two teachers into several study halls. Small groups get extra help from each teacher for 20 minutes a day during that period. Sandburg Middle School uses frontloading, which are 10-minute sneak previews of vocabulary and concepts that will be introduced to the whole class later. Sometimes a special education teacher or an aide does this with small groups in the classroom, and sometimes the classroom teacher does it while the class works on another assignment. This mini-lesson provides extra instructional time for Tier 2 students before they experience failure.

Kyle: Don't kids who receive frontloading fall behind on what the rest of the class is doing? I can't imagine that those students will be cooperative if they have more homework because their teacher substituted group instruction for work time.

Sandra: You're right. We all need to accept the fact that every assignment isn't golden. Struggling students don't need more work weighing them down. Frontloading is more effective replacement work for material that the teacher deems less critical for that particular group. Cutting out part of the assignment and giving credit for the carefully modeled and guided work done in small groups on the same skills is fair and smart.

Kyle: That makes sense. Any other options?

Sandra: Yes, Marshall Middle School schedules a 30-minute Intervention/Enrichment period. My brother teaches 7th grade there and his I/E period is right after lunch. All 7th grade teachers, plus a tutor, a special education teacher, an aide, a counselor, and one of the administrators, take a group or two based on a common need. Instructors work with these groups for four weeks on their targeted skills, and then they regroup kids based on a new set of needs.

Kyle: The Marshall plan sounds like one that could work here if we could schedule it. Do the teachers like that arrangement?

Sandra: They did for the first three months, but two of the teachers let the period deteriorate into a study hall. The rest of the team is furious and, word is, they're on the warpath. I'll keep you updated.

This school's problem with fidelity of implementation is not uncommon. I often see administrators schedule a daily intervention period to give kids a "double dose" of instruction only to see this well-intended effort devolve into yet another study hall. This problem tends to occur when the program has a weak structure or there is a lack of clear expectations about monitoring and what Tier 2 should be. Quality training, clear procedures, and scheduled time to evaluate results have to be built into the RTI process.

Tier 2 structure and criteria

It is important to reiterate that Tier 1 instruction is the first line of defense. However, if a student is more than a year below grade-level expectations, Tier 2 support should start as soon as possible. The Tier 2 formula for successful small-group intervention is to use modeling, active participation, corrective feedback, self-monitoring, practice to mastery, and efficient time on task in every session. This approach works for both academic skills and behavior. Teams that establish specific sets of highly active research-based strategies not only see good results but also remove the burden of solo planning from teachers.

Tier 2 instruction needs

- Systematic and explicit instruction that includes modeling and direct teaching.
- Specialized programming that focuses on just a few key skills at a time.
- Frontloading of skills to be introduced at a later time in the general education class.
- A variety of practice opportunities that coordinate with identified classroom skills but use different approaches.
- Continuous corrective feedback, encouragement, and self-monitoring activities.
- Weekly progress monitoring and charting to check growth patterns.

Tier 2 is typically implemented with groups of three to six students who have similar skill needs. Sessions last 10–45 minutes and are done at least three times a week. Sometimes Tier 2 strategies are delivered within the general education classroom as quick, small-group reteaching and reinforcement lessons; sometimes they are delivered during intervention periods outside the core classroom. No matter how long the session is, where it is held, or who conducts it, following a well-defined daily routine of fast-paced activities is the key to success. Success is defined as adequate student progress along the established goal line (as described in Chapter 4).

For example, 2nd grade students who are struggling with similar reading and writing skills should be scheduled into an intervention group that meets for 30 minutes three times a week. The intervention sessions address the five key components (according to Reading First research) of quality language arts instruction: fluency, phonics, vocabulary, phonemic awareness, and comprehension (U.S. Department of Health and Human

Services, 2000). A daily rapid routine at the elementary level might look something like this:

- Students simultaneously read aloud (three minutes).
- Students use magnetic letters to practice phonics skills that match the general education lessons (two minutes).
- Partners read vocabulary words aloud to each other (two minutes).
- Students clap out syllables together (one minute).
- Students write dictated words in syllables (two minutes).
- The teacher models a comprehension strategy using a "think aloud" strategy (three minutes).
- Students read a passage aloud and apply the new strategy (two minutes).
- Partners retell the story to each other (one minute).
- Students write a summary of their story in their journals (three minutes).

In each of these steps, all Tier 2 group members simultaneously perform their tasks. This keeps every student actively involved throughout the fast-paced session, unlike a round-robin approach to reading. The teacher is also able to listen in and provide individualized corrective feedback for each student.

Procedures should be followed daily, thus creating a routine so familiar that the students are able to intuitively follow the lessons with little time wasted to explaining basic directions. Familiar routines also reinforce previously taught skills while modeling and teaching new ones. The skills can be altered to reflect specific student needs or relevant skills, based on material emphasized in the classroom.

Pace and involvement of Tier 2 intervention sessions at a secondary level are very similar to the elementary level. Direct vocabulary instruction in a variety of contexts and modeling of specific strategies are both essential components of Tier 2 intervention at any level. A rapid routine for secondary schools might look something like this:

- Students practice vocabulary in context (two minutes).
- Students connect the text to existing background knowledge (three minutes).
- Teachers read aloud and model comprehension strategies and marking text (i.e., sticky notes, highlighting, margin writing) (four minutes).
- Students practice the modeled strategy while they read silently (four minutes).
- Students compare text markings (three minutes).
- Students organize their information on a graphic organizer (three minutes).
- Students write summaries in their journals (four minutes).
- Students engage in spelling and word segmentation activities (three minutes).

Tier 2 instruction is intended to provide 20–30 sessions of supplemental intervention, lasting from six to nine weeks. The problem-solving team (which includes classroom teachers) then analyzes the student data and makes a decision to

- Support the student using only Tier 1 interventions.
- Continue Tier 2 support with some new strategies.
- Increase the intervention intensity by moving to a Tier 3 plan.

Finding time for Tier 2

Small-group tutoring during the school day is hard to schedule, especially in most middle and high schools. Teachers often meet resistance from students who prefer not to be singled out. With this in mind, options such as before- or after-school programs, special elective courses, and coteaching should be considered as viable alternatives for Tier 2 intervention sessions.

Classroom teachers often provide their own Tier 2 interventions by conducting 10- or 15-minute minilessons while the rest of the class is working on practice or extension work. Specially trained noncertified personnel can also implement carefully scripted or computer-based programs within or outside the general education classroom. Sometimes, gifted, ESL, Title I, or special education teachers/tutors come into a class to conduct minilessons after the main instruction is complete and while the general education teacher is conducting small-group work or individual student conferences.

Teachers often ask how to schedule the Tier 2 "double doses" without interfering with Tier 1 instruction. It is critical that supplementary interventions—whether they are delivered in the general education classroom or as a pull-out option— do not prevent students from receiving the direct instruction associated with a lesson in a general education room. The following situation is an example of how this might play out in a classroom.

It is critical that supplementary interventions do not prevent students from receiving direct instruction in the general education room.

Mrs. Spain is an intervention specialist who coteaches with Mr. Adams during second period. After Mrs. Spain introduces the lesson, Mr. Adams proceeds with 25 minutes of direct teaching, and he periodically pauses for reflection and note taking. The class is then given an assignment, at which point Mrs. Spain initiates a Tier 2 intervention session with five students. She sits with these students in a small group and goes over material with which they need further support and that matches Mr. Adams's core instruction. As the Tier 2 students meet and the rest of the class completes the assignment, Mr. Adams takes the opportunity to give individual feedback or conduct a separate small-group activity (perhaps a group that needs enrichment or extension). Both teachers finish in time to summarize the day's material and preview the next day's work.

Whenever I give this example, teachers often ask, "When do the students in the small groups do the class assignment?" The answer? They often don't. This is where pacing and task differentiation factors in. General education teachers must accept the fact that not every assignment is critical. If the small-group and whole-class tasks are truly coordinated, work done in small groups (when conducted with fidelity) can be a suitable replacement for what the rest of the class does independently. The intervention session can also be a better use of Tier 2 students' time than the independent assignment would have been. Importantly, the small-group activity should never be just a worksheet; it should always contain modeling and practice using "I do; We do; You do" instruction.

Some schools establish special Intervention and Enrichment periods each day to address Tier 2 students' needs. In this situation, each department or grade level usually partners with another department or grade level to schedule a joint intervention period (e.g., grades 1 and 2, grades 3 and 4, grades 5 and 6). This potentially frees up numerous teachers during the shared intervention period (even more if specialists join in). By thinking beyond their grade-level boundaries, teachers are able to group and regroup students in a variety of ways based upon skill readiness, interest areas, matched partners, and so forth. Students on the watch list often attend Tier 2 skill recovery sessions or sessions that preteach skills that are going to be introduced in general education classes later in the week. Students with enrichment and extension needs will have the time and opportunity to explore new areas not able to be covered in a general education class.

HOW TO ... *maintain flexibility*

Teachers should regard pyramid intervention strategies and programs as flexible tools used to adjust the intensity of instruction as a student's growth pattern fluctuates. Students who start in Tier 2 move to Tier 1 once their achievement pattern indicates less need for rigorous support. This flexibility provides a timely response when a student hits a temporary plateau and needs to return to Tier 2 for a time. This flexibility also avoids the kind of oversupport that creates "learned helplessness" often found in students who have been given too many accommodations or have been allowed to hold onto these crutches for too long.

Tier 3 Intensive Intervention

Tier 3 is the most intense level of intervention on the continuum of pyramid options. At Tier 3, the goal is remediation of existing academic, social, or emotional problems and prevention of more severe problems. Chronic nonresponders to Tier 1 instruction and Tier 2 support are candidates for these Tier 3 intensive interventions.

It is possible that some students may have learning gaps so severe that the problem-solving team will recommend Tier 3 interventions without first trying Tier 2 support. Districts need to independently establish specific criteria for which students will be served at each tier. There is a considerable increase in intensity with Tier 3 interventions, namely:

> Districts need to establish specific criteria for identifying which students will be served at each tier.

- Group size is only one to three students.
- Time per week is 150–300 minutes.
- Duration is 9–12 weeks.
- Progress monitoring is conducted up to twice a week.
- Level of intensity generally requires a full period of instruction held outside a general education classroom.
- Educator responsible for intervention sessions requires specialized training (e.g., Title I reading teacher, psychologist, counselor, special education teacher, therapist, highly trained aide using a scripted program).

Tier 3 structure and criteria

Like Tier 2, daily Tier 3 lessons need to be fast paced with good modeling followed by very focused guided practice. Ongoing positive corrective feedback is needed to keep student interest and involvement high. These lessons are more intense because of the smaller group size and longer sessions. Independent worksheets are minimized because active instruction is what these students need. The class routine needs to be so familiar that students are able to follow the lessons with little time wasted explaining basic directions. Lessons will reinforce old skills while modeling and teaching new ones.

Tier 3 instruction needs

- Systematic and explicit instruction that includes modeling and direct teaching using multiple examples.
- Specialized programming that focuses on just a few key skills at a time.
- Mirroring of skills being taught in the general education classroom, as well as attention to filling in skill gaps that are causing difficulty in the general education classroom.
- A variety of practice opportunities that coordinate with identified classroom skills but use different approaches.
- Continuous corrective feedback, encouragement, and self-monitoring activities.

At Tier 3, students who are two or more years below grade level need highly individualized instruction and support four or five times per week. These sessions often utilize intensive research-based programs to target the exact weaknesses of particular students.

For example, a student who has had an extended period of illness might fall behind by an entire grade level. One or two nine-week Tier 3 sessions may bring the skill level close to grade level if the classroom and Tier 3 teacher carefully plan for this transition. In this manner, students sometimes return to Tier 1 without bridging through Tier 2.

Tier 3 interventions—like Tier 2—must incorporate opportunities to transfer new skills to the general education setting. The card shown in Figure 5.2 is an example of a specific strategy that can be used daily with two or three students, with the ultimate goal of moving them up to Tier 2. Tier 3—again, like Tier 2—is not a replacement for Tier 1 instruction. Therefore, strategies such as this should enable students to successfully apply knowledge and skills in the general education classroom with few (or no) supplemental supports from the teacher.

Tier 3 utilizes intensive research-based programs to target the exact weaknesses of particular students.

Figure 5.2 | Pyramid Card, Sample 2

Teacher: Hillary West

Appropriate for Grade Levels: K–12

Date: December 2010

Intervention: Think-Aloud Strategy—This intervention is designed to teach self-management and social skills, independence, consequence anticipation, option consideration, and self-evaluation. It can be used at Tier 3.

Materials: social skills cards with role-play situations; cueing card with problem-solving steps; two trained adults

Frequency and Duration: 20 minutes daily for three to four months, depending upon student's willingness to respond

Instructional Steps (conduct these steps every day):
1. TEACHER MODELING AND ROLE-PLAY: Role-play problem scenarios with a coteacher or aide. Model the targeted process using a first-person "think-aloud" approach to briefly describe the problem and consider options, required steps, and things you might want to avoid. Explain your rationale and then arrive at a decision.

2. PRACTICE: Have students role-play a similar situation and conduct their thinking aloud.

3. ERROR CORRECTION: Role-play a new situation with a coteacher or aide and have students identify flaws in how the adults used the procedure.

4 PRACTICE: Students should practice increasingly complex situations using these procedural steps both within and outside the small-group setting.

Figure 5.2	**Pyramid Card, Sample 2 (cont.)**

Progress Monitoring: Gather and chart data that illustrate an increase in specific new behaviors and a reduction in the frequency of unfavorable behaviors. Students can also conduct daily self-monitoring activities using prescribed questions.

Research Basis: Curwin, R. L., Mendler, A. N., & Mendler, B. D. (2008). *Discipline with dignity: New challenges, new solutions* (3rd ed.). Alexandria, VA: ASCD.

Teacher Comments:

After 9–12 weeks of intensive Tier 3 intervention, the problem-solving team (which includes the classroom teachers) analyzes the student data and makes a decision to

- Support the student using only Tier 1 and Tier 2 intervention if the Tier 3 strategies have been successful.
- Recommend continuing Tier 3 instruction using new strategies if the student is showing growth but not closing the academic or behavior gap.
- Recommend formal evaluation procedures for special education while continuing new Tier 3 strategies if Tier 3 intervention is unsuccessful.

HOW TO . . . *make Tier 3 interventions work*

Skills acquired during Tier 3 intervention sessions must be practiced and reinforced in Tiers 1 and 2 to ensure that a seamless transfer of learning takes place. This requires communication and collaboration among everyone involved.

Finding time for Tier 3

Tier 3 is generally a double class taken as an elective. For instance, a student behind in reading may take the regular

English class as well as an additional reading or writing class. A student failing his or her chemistry class can sit in on the chemistry class for a second time during a study hall later in the day until the double dose is no longer needed.

Tier 3 in the elementary grades is often scheduled by splitting the 90-minute language arts block into 45 minutes of language arts in the general education room and 45 minutes in a specialized reading program. This needs to be carefully orchestrated so pull-out time happens when the rest of the group is doing independent or small-group work. This minimizes the loss of general education instruction for Tier 3 students.

It is common to find elementary and middle schools scheduling a 30- to 45-minute intervention/enrichment period daily. A Tier 3–level instruction class would typically require attendance daily instead of the two or three sessions a week in Tier 2. Tier 3 support classes are often offered before and after school, in addition to summer school intervention classes.

What If Students Still Don't Learn?

If progress data indicate that students are not actively closing the achievement gap, the first response is generally to try a different instructional strategy. If the problem persists, you will need to check for fidelity of implementation. Does the teacher need a mentor or professional development in order to adjust the delivery of the strategy? If the instructional strategies and fidelity of implementation are not the problem, then you might have a student with a learning disability.

Students who do not respond to targeted research-based interventions over an extended period of time are then considered for eligibility for special education services as required by the Individuals with Disabilities Education Act. Data collected during Tiers 1, 2, and 3 become part of the multifactored evaluation (i.e., an in-depth analysis of psychological and educational functioning) and are used in conjunction with other data to make eligibility decisions. It is common for 5 percent of all students (approximately one per class) to require Tier 3 intensive interventions in order to be successful, and some of these students will qualify for special education services (Batch et al., 2006).

If the number of students who require Tier 3 interventions exceeds 5 percent, consider alternative ways to strengthen the prevention efforts of Tiers 1 and 2. Avoid the temptation of allowing too many students to enter Tier 3 just because it is "strong medicine." Resources are limited, and it is important not to spread them so thinly that they become ineffective.

Avoid the temptation of allowing too many students to enter Tier 3 just because it is "strong medicine."

Summary

Each tier on the pyramid of interventions provides a safety net to catch students who are at risk of slipping through the cracks. At Tier 1, teachers use research-based instruction to guard against practices that yield low results. Tier 2 provides a "double dose" of instruction and support to help students who perform below grade level. Tier 3 is a longer, more intense version of Tier 2 that is designed to close learning gaps for students who perform significantly below grade level.

This pyramid of support cannot work without a comprehensive database of the best available practices, a systematic monitoring of the effectiveness of these practices, and ongoing instructional adjustments based on students' responses to interventions. The database, along with support from the problem-solving team, helps teachers answer the question "If this isn't working, what will?"

In the next chapter, we will look at specific Tier 1 strategies that, if used consistently, can reduce the number of students who need intensive interventions.

6

Prevention Is More Efficient Than Cure

Response to Intervention, as a term, suits Tier 2 and Tier 3 perfectly because they focus on intervention systems that close learning gaps. Tier 1, however, is more of a "response to instruction" since it focuses on quality instruction required to prevent the gaps from occurring in the first place. If 80–90 percent of the students' needs are being met using only Tier 1 general education instruction, then you know you have a healthy curriculum and instructional system in place. Successful Tier 1 instruction, then, is defined by few students ever needing more intense interventions.

Unfortunately, there is no one set of magical strategies or programs that creates perfect classroom instruction. A strategy that works beautifully for one teacher may fall flat for another. A highly effective strategy for one student may have no impact on another. Research does verify that some fundamental aspects of instruction, when implemented systematically and with fidelity, make a big difference in student achievement and behavior (Marzano, Pickering, & Pollock, 2001). This chapter focuses on six research-based strategies that are proven to increase success for general education, gifted, and struggling learners.

Six Areas of Prevention

Two teachers recently asked me, "If you were the queen of this district, what six changes would you make to reduce the number of struggling kids?" I thought about that for weeks. The changes would have to solve problems shared by every grade in every school, and the results would have to be worth the effort. I would also need strategies proven effective with a majority of students in a wide variety of circumstances. Any response that adequately meets these criteria forms the framework of a solid Tier 1 plan. My advice to you—as it was to those teachers—is to start with the six areas of prevention discussed in this chapter (see Figure 6.1) to refine and perfect Tier 1 instruction according to the unique requirements of your district.

Figure 6.1 | **Six Areas of Prevention**

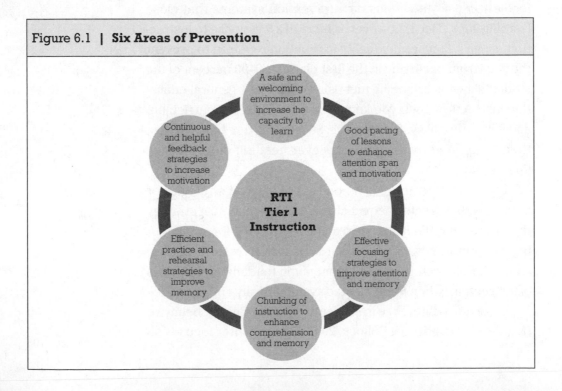

A Safe and Welcoming Environment

Research shows that the more stress and anxiety a person experiences, the harder it is to learn. The longer this negative stress persists, the more debilitating it becomes (Wolfe, 2001). Student stress in schools is caused by things like bullying, harsh criticism, rejection, fear of looking stupid in front of friends, and feeling academically overwhelmed, to name just a few. This anxiety causes students to focus more on social survival than academics. Teachers need strategies that minimize these negative effects of stress and help students feel safe and welcome in school no matter what their lives might be like outside school. I will describe five key and closely related areas that can make your building feel safe and welcome: emotional safety, respect, relevance, relationships, and academic safety.

Emotional safety

Students feel emotionally safe when their environment is fair, flexible, and predictable. To create a fair and predictable environment, teachers establish clear classroom routines, rules, and procedures to reduce classroom disruptions and increase attention to task (Marzano, Marzano, & Pickering, 2003). Effective teachers limit the number of rules and explain the rationale behind them. They also provide opportunities for student input so students can recognize and understand the need for these guidelines. Research demonstrates that ground rules in student-centered classrooms have built-in flexibility so different strategies can be used for different types of students, but consistent expectations for all students are maintained (Brophy & McCaslin, 1992).

A safe environment is fair, flexible, and predictable.

I once worked with a 3rd grade teacher, Elaine, who had one of the calmest and most respectful classrooms I have ever seen. Her techniques could work at every grade level. The following vignette shows how she established a firm but friendly tone in her classroom.

HOW TO . . . *establish effective classroom management*

1. Decide upon five or six basic expectations that help students feel accepted and safe.
2. Involve students in establishing and clarifying rules.
3. Take time to model and teach routines so students internalize expectations.
4. Reteach routines and procedures regularly so they become automatic.
5. Be consistent and fair in enforcing rules, but also be flexible in order to meet individual needs.

On the first day of school Elaine laid out three expectations:

- Everyone must be able to concentrate on his or her own work.
- No one should ever feel embarrassed, put down, or unsafe.
- Everyone needs to take care of the classroom, materials, and supplies.

Then Elaine asked, "What class rules should we set up to make sure these things happen?" From the first day of school, she made it clear that every member of the class contributed to running the classroom. She didn't give her students carte blanche, but she did establish joint ownership for maintaining a healthy and orderly environment.

Elaine was also very precise in describing, modeling, and following through on the steps for every procedure she established. For example, students wrote their assigned numbers on the top right corner of every paper, and then numerically arranged their work in the "completed" folder. Elaine explained, "This lets me quickly see if you forgot to hand in your assignment before you leave class. We can also save time with attendance by just counting off each morning. During a fire drill we can count off and know immediately who may not be safe."

These are the types of procedures and routines that make a classroom feel fair, flexible, and predictable.

Besides helping students recognize the usefulness of classroom routines, teachers should also consider reteaching two routines every day. This takes only a minute or two each day, but it saves hours of valuable instructional time (Smith, 2004). Teachers who establish clear and consistent guidelines for carrying out basic classroom tasks have classrooms that run efficiently. In your school, consider the routines and expectations for

- Coming into the room and starting work quickly.
- Taking attendance and lunch count.
- Collecting fees.
- Distributing and collecting assignments, material, and supplies.
- Making clear transitions from one activity to another (e.g., moving to a different part of the classroom, moving furniture to create small-group work areas, clearing desks, lining up).
- Establishing guidelines for participation or asking questions (e.g., raising hands, working in groups).
- Creating effective methods to get the group's attention (e.g., lights, music).
- Expressing concerns about and identifying resolutions to issues.
- Dedicating time to classroom cleaning and dismissal.

These may seem like commonsense procedures, but teachers with chaotic classrooms often underestimate the power of teaching and maintaining precise routines. Predictable rituals protect instructional time and create a calm, safe feeling for students, but we must go further than that. To be truly effective, districts and schools must develop the social safety of a caring community.

Respect

The Canada Employment and Immigration Commission interviewed 5,000 high school dropouts about why they left school. Answers focused on the "three *R*s"—students didn't feel *respected*, learning wasn't *relevant*, and *relationships* with teachers and peers weren't meaningful (Van der Klift & Kunc, 2009). Researchers heard statements such as "No one knows who I am and they really don't care. They only care about the work being handed in on time."

There are more ways to drop out than walk away from school. Kindergarten children who feel overwhelmed and alone may just sit down and cry. Fourth graders who feel left out and confused may daydream or rebel. Middle school students who are ignored or no longer consider themselves capable simply say, "School is lame." High school students who feel disrespected by academics, grading systems, or other people may just walk out. In all of these cases, learning effectively shuts down. However, an ounce of prevention can reduce all of these dropout problems. Here is a helpful "to-do list" for maintaining a respectful environment in school:

- Create classrooms that are user-friendly, organized, and pleasant work environments where teachers genuinely believe that struggling students are capable of learning, given the right conditions and strategies. Research shows that students reflect the negative or positive attitudes of their teachers (Sanders & Rivers, 1996).
- Encourage risk taking by avoiding criticism of genuine efforts, even when the effort is off target and misses the mark. Give recognition for any part of an answer that is right, or credit the student for answering a different question. For example, say, "I think you just answered 2 + 4, and you were right. What I asked for was 2 × 4. Can you do that one?"

Respect, relevant learning, and meaningful relationships help create a safe and welcoming academic environment.

- Avoid using grades as punishment. Allow students several practice assignments to work out difficulties and confusion before taking grades. Until a student proves competence in an area, work lower than a *C* can be redone or revised until this benchmark is achieved. Beginning learners of every age need encouragement and support to succeed at new skills. Teachers often fear that students will procrastinate and have a poor work ethic under this system, but research proves that this method is highly likely to increase student responsibility and achievement levels (Reeves, 2006).
- Teach relaxation techniques for students to use when they are tense or wound up, rather than wait until they make poor choices and get in trouble. The ability to calm oneself down while under pressure is an important life skill to teach.
- Assign respectful work that neither insults students' intelligence with busywork nor pushes them to a frustration level that is unhealthy.

Relevance

Relevance helps students recognize and appreciate the purpose and usefulness of a lesson or rule. If relevance is lacking, students often have a hard time remembering and complying with classroom routines. It's like their brains are surfing the Internet for information but not picking up on anything interesting enough to latch on to. As a result, motivation and focus dwindles.

The following sections introduce four ways to create a strong sense of relevance; two are related to academics (choices and linking to prior knowledge), and two are intended to improve behavior (logical consequences and collaborative problem solving).

Choices

Research shows that providing choices increases task engagement and lowers disruptive behavior for students with disabilities (Powell & Nelson, 1997). The ability to make independent academic choices provides students with a sense of control and power, and it can be implemented without giving away the educational "farm." Simply ask, "Do you want to work alone or together; at your desk or at the table; on math or reading first?" Allowing students to choose topics that interest them generally makes assignments more palatable. Giving students choices for demonstrating how well they know the skills and concepts taught can make life more interesting for both teachers and students.

I once had a student teacher who did not understand that these assessment options should hold to a common standard of mastery. She complained, "The kids always choose the easy one." The first question she needed to ask herself, however, was "Why did I offer them the choice of an easy assessment?" It's important to remember that all assessment choices should measure the same level of competence. The target doesn't change, but the way students choose to demonstrate competence may. The following example illustrates this point.

You are enrolled in my RTI course, and there will be an RTI assessment tomorrow. I give you four options to demonstrate what you know: (1) write a paper on RTI; (2) prepare an RTI presentation for the whole group; (3) design a flowchart showing how the RTI components flow together, and explain that chart to a small group; or (4) perform a series of skits showing the components of RTI and how they work together. No matter which assessment method you select, the scoring rubric addresses the same concepts to clarify, vocabulary to explain, and relationships to demonstrate. Performing the skit may be more appealing to you than writing a paper—and therefore seem easier—but your assessment criteria will not be less demanding, nor will they measure different material.

Another way to win cooperation and encourage a sense of relevance is to allow students to choose which parts of an assignment to complete. For example, in one of my classes, all I had to say was "You do not have to do the entire assignment unless you want to. You may eliminate any three questions, except those that I indicated are mandatory." Because they wanted to be sure to eliminate the "hardest" questions, my students read every question more carefully than they normally would have.

Linking to prior knowledge

Robert Marzano's research shows that identifying similarities and differences to prior knowledge is the core to all learning (Marzano & Pickering, 2001). Making connections to prior knowledge is critical in every subject area. Effective teachers intentionally make links in every lesson through strategies such as analogies, stories, graphic organizers, and authentic application activities. These strategies, however, should be used as linking tools. Simply asking students to use a graphic organizer, for example, is not proven to be an effective practice. Graphic organizers improve learning only when teachers also incorporate explicit instruction, modeling, and independent practice with feedback (Gardill & Jitendra, 1999). Figure 6.2 presents an activity—like one you might use in your pyramid of interventions database—for making connections to any new concept.

> Relevance is enhanced by helping students connect new ideas to their prior knowledge.

Logical consequences

William Glasser refers to common errors that teachers make when responding to student discipline problems as "The Seven Deadly Habits": criticizing, blaming, complaining, nagging, threatening, punishing, and bribing (Glasser, 1992). In response

---

Figure 6.2 | Pyramid Card, Sample 3

Teacher: Phil Roth

Appropriate for Grade Levels: 4–12

Date: December 2010

Intervention: Analogy Matrix—This intervention teaches comparing and contrasting, linking to prior knowledge, summarizing, identifying similarities and differences, and making analogies. It can be used with large or small groups at any tier.

Materials: student copies of a three-column chart with the categories: *Something I Know About, What I'm Learning About, Things They Have in Common;* chalkboard or projector; sticky notes or index cards

Frequency and Duration: Use when deep understanding of a topic is important but difficult to grasp. Use four times a week for two weeks in various content areas. Use at least once a week after that until the procedure is internalized.

Instructional Steps:

1. FOCUS TASK: Explain that students are to look for patterns that exist between what they know and what they need to know. Display the chart and explain that it is very similar to a Venn diagram, with which students should already be familiar (if necessary, draw a Venn diagram on the board and review how it is used to compare and contrast two objects or concepts). Write the name of the familiar topic on the left side of the chart and the name of a new topic on the right side (e.g., *roads and highways* [familiar topic] and *circulatory system* [new topic]).

2. BRAINSTORM: Have the class generate a list of important ideas for the familiar topic. Write them on sticky notes and place them in the left column. Write only helpful traits that link to the new topic. For example:

Something I Know About	Things They Have in Common	What I'm Learning About
roads and highways		*circulatory system*
carry vehicles	both transport material	carries blood
need constant repair and repaving	both need routine care and maintenance	needs a healthy diet to work well
big roads lead to smaller roads	both are systems of connected pathways	large vessels connect to smaller vessels
Summary:		

As the lesson progresses, use the right column on the chart to list features of the unknown concept that match each of those in the known concept column (e.g., "carries blood" matches "carry vehicles"). Help students describe what both concepts have in common, and write these shared attributes in the middle column (e.g. "both transport material").

3. SUMMARIZE: Ask students to write their own definition of the new topic, incorporating all the common-pattern sticky notes in their definition.

Progress Monitoring: Have students repeat this process, using a different set of topics.

Research Basis: Deshler, D., Schumaker, J., Bulgren, J., Lenz, K., Jantzen, J., Adams, G., . . . Marquis, J. (2001). Making learning easier: Connecting new knowledge to things students already know. *TEACHING Exceptional Children, 33*(4), 82–85.
Wormeli, R. (2005). *Summarization in any subject.* Alexandria, VA: ASCD.

Teacher Comments: After modeling this strategy multiple times, I have the students fill in the left column as a class brainstorm and the right column as they read the text. I then have the kids list the shared traits rather than tell them what to look for.

to a behavior problem, many adults' first impulse is to punish or confiscate a valued possession or privilege. However, this approach is prone to backfiring, unless it is a consequence that fits the crime. For example, if a child uses equipment inappropriately, forbidding him to use that equipment for a while—unless properly supervised—is a logical consequence. Sending him to the principal's office, though, is not logically connected to the offense and, therefore, not a practical response. If a student fails to complete an assignment, a logical consequence might be to have her do it at a time that is less convenient for her; a zero in the grade book is not a logical response and does not teach her to assume responsibility or to take ownership for her actions.

Collaborative problem solving

Ross Greene's research shows that repeated violations of a rule or procedure aren't always an indication that a child is choosing to defy (Greene, 2008). Infractions often represent a student's delay in developing the skill to critically think through problems and see the relevance of suggested solutions. Many times, adults develop strategies to help a student improve academically or behaviorally, but the student may see these plans as simply more rules to follow rather than as ways to reach a goal. One way to help students see the relevance of an idea is to involve them in designing the plan together.

Negotiation of behavior solutions has three steps: empathy for the situation, definition of the problem, and collaboration to identify possible solutions.

- Use empathy to keep the student calm and put his or her concern on the table.
- Define the problem from your point of view without talking about the solution.
- Invite the student to help brainstorm a list of potential solutions before deciding on a realistic and mutually satisfying solution.

This approach takes dedication and persistence, and it is not an easy answer. However, the positive effects are supported by years of research from Harvard Medical School (Greene, 2008). In my own experience, I have found the following guidelines to be very helpful for conducting problem-solving conferences:

- Schedule proactive conferences with students who regularly make poor choices. Don't wait until you are in the "heat of battle" to address alternative choices.
- Ensure that the student has seen a list of negotiable and nonnegotiable issues before you schedule this conference. Familiarity with and understanding of these issues—before the meeting—is often key to success.
- Define the desired behaviors, with student input, and list possibilities for achieving them.
- Avoid rejecting any student ideas during the brainstorming process, no matter how absurd. Focus on constructive listening, and be prepared to make compromises. Agree to as many student ideas as possible, but don't be afraid to draw the line on important issues. If you come to an impasse, agree to reopen talks in a day or two.

- Have the student explain the final agreement—one that describes the rule and consequence with which you can both live—in his or her own words. Reread aloud your written notes on the agreement and the specific criteria for judging acceptable follow-through.
- Sign and date the agreement to avoid the potential confrontation with a student who claims, "I didn't agree to that."

Don't expect behavior to change overnight. If the student violates the agreement, your responsibility is to follow through with the agreed-upon consequence quickly—but calmly—and let the student know that he or she will be given another chance to adhere to the agreement.

Relationships

In classrooms where high standards and good relationships are the norm, students are more likely to accept their responsibility to cooperate, respect themselves and others, and give high energy to learning (Kohl, 1994). Safe and welcoming classrooms build both respectful teacher-to-student and student-to-student relationships. ·

Relationships with teachers

Have you ever seen a student act out in one class but never dream of causing a disturbance in the next class? There is a reason for this change. By virtue of their status, all teachers have position power; that is, the power to bestow rewards and dole out consequences. Some teachers also have personal power: the power earned through respect and trust. You can instantly tell which power base teachers operate from by observing student behavior in the classroom.

Teachers who rely totally on their position power to make students behave often find themselves fighting regular discipline

Position power is connected to a teacher's authority to reward and punish; personal power is earned through respect.

battles. Students are more likely to misbehave and be disrespectful to teachers they dislike and cannot relate to, therefore achievement and motivation are generally lower in these classrooms. Teachers build personal power by doing things that show genuine respect for and interest in their students. Some specific examples include

- Being fair, firm, and consistent in enforcing expectations.
- Following through on promises.
- Making a sincere effort to learn about students' interests, viewpoints, and talents.
- Maintaining an upbeat and friendly environment by doing things such as greeting students at the door, asking for students' opinions, showing a sense of humor, and protecting students' dignity by not embarrassing them in front of others.
- Incorporating fun into every class period without sacrificing instructional rigor.
- Setting high expectations for behavior and achievement that stretch students to meet their potential while delivering the kinds of support that make meeting those high expectations possible.
- Making time to be a good listener and being gracious enough to apologize to students when you make a mistake.
- Providing clear feedback and opportunities to redo work so students learn from their mistakes.

HOW TO . . . *calculate your personal power*

Imagine that you have a personal emotional bank account with each student. Visualize every criticism as a withdrawal and every positive interaction as a deposit. One criticism erases 12 caring and positive deposits. Emotional accounts that go into the red reduce your power to motivate and influence a learner (Purkey & Novak, 1996).

Relationships among classmates

Unfortunately, there are often cases where students feel excluded from and alienated by peers and teachers. Everyone, even a teen with a surly exterior, wants to be respected by and connected to both adults and peers. When this connection doesn't happen, it erodes motivation. Ginsberg and Wlodkowski (2000) list the research behind and strategies for helping students feel included and respected in culturally responsive classrooms:

- Create activities for sharing ideas and opinions in a variety of different groupings while respecting the student's right to privacy by building in a "pass" option during group discussions.
- Help students learn each other's names and share things they have in common (e.g., music, travel, dislikes, favorite foods).
- Build activities into lessons that reduce stereotyping and bias by teaching ways people with different beliefs and backgrounds share the same needs, feelings, and experiences.
- Refuse to take part in or allow put-downs of any type.
- Ensure everyone is recognized for the strengths they each bring to class.

You can be masterful in content knowledge and strategies, but if you do not have the ability to connect with students, you will never be effective as a teacher of academics or behavior. This ability to connect is the linchpin for making all other strategies work.

Academic safety

When Henry Ford informed his engineers that he wanted them to design a V-8 engine, the engineers told him it couldn't be done. Henry Ford reportedly said, "If you think you can or think you can't, either way you're right. Now I'll give you 90 days to do the job." After 90 days of convincing themselves they were right, the engineers came back with proof that the V-8 engine was impossible to build. Ford refused to accept that proof and made them continue the work. His optimism eventually trumped the engineers' pessimism, demonstrating that well-founded beliefs play a major role in creating reality.

High expectations for low-performing students are critical to their academic and behavioral success.

Research conducted by agencies such as the Manhattan Institute, the University of New Mexico, and the Center for Research on the Education of Students Placed at Risk have all found that high expectations for low-performing students are critical to their own "can-do" attitudes (Barr & Parrett, 2007).

Beliefs and expectations not only have a huge impact on student learning and behavior but also influence a teacher's treatment of students. I have often heard teachers claim that they had high expectations, but they were only referring to students they already deemed to be capable. Those same teachers have also made statements such as "Let's be realistic—he's special ed" or "Have you met her mom? She's a piece of work, so what can you expect?" This is a perfect example of the kind of "stinking thinking" that dooms kids to low achievement and low self-esteem.

Research shows that teachers treat low performers differently than high performers. According to Marzano (2007), low performers

- Receive less praise for their successes.
- Are seated farther from the teacher.
- Receive fewer smiles, fewer friendly remarks, and less positive nonverbal attention.
- Are given less wait time to answer and are called upon less frequently.
- Are given more answers and receive less informative feedback.
- Have lower demands.

- Are given fewer effective strategies for improvement when time is short.

Marzano's recommendation for correcting this pattern of behavior is to make a list of students who are perceived to be low performers and monitor the behaviors listed above. In essence, awareness of the problem is half of the solution. The other half is to intentionally reverse each of these nonproductive patterns. Make more eye contact, purposely engage students in friendly conversations, and give credit for parts of answers that students get right.

High expectations are not helpful, however, if they are not supported by appropriate safety nets and scaffolds. Research shows that scaffolding can minimize frustration and increase time on task by clarifying the purpose and steps of a learning situation (McKenzie, 2000).

Scaffolding provides assistance and structure until students can independently solve the problem or do the work. Examples of scaffolding include cueing, graphic organizers, step-by-step directions, guiding questions, think-aloud modeling, rubrics, cooperative learning, and technology. Scaffolding, though, should only be a temporary crutch that helps learners feel academically safe.[1]

If overused, scaffolding creates learned helplessness. If scaffolding is not provided, learning can appear to be an impossible task and motivation is lost. It is therefore important to gradually withdraw scaffolding in order to strike a balance between too much help and not enough. Here are a few ways to scaffold a struggling reader in any content area:

- Check the readability of material. If the readability is too high, find a replacement resource that presents similar information.

> Scaffolding can minimize student frustration and increase time on task.

> If overused, scaffolding creates learned helplessness.

---

[1] A great reference for scaffolding ideas, reading interventions, and accommodations is the Florida Center for Reading Research Web site (www.fcrr.org).

- Utilize text-to-speech software that has the ability to read aloud digital text. A computer and a pair of earphones can make a science textbook accessible to a student reading several years below grade level. Free software downloads are available from several Web sites, as are fancier and more expensive commercial programs.[2]

- Change the font size, color, and type in digital text. Students sometimes become overwhelmed by the density of print on a page. Better spacing between lines can also make an apparently daunting text seem manageable.

- Experiment with printing assignments on colored paper. Color helps some readers, and print is sometimes easier to read with contrasting background colors.

- Add subtitles, charts, pictures, and graphs to texts. Graphics and subtitles not only break up blocks of print but can provide readers with clues that aid comprehension.

Instructional Pacing

The tempo at which teachers proceed has a huge effect on student learning. If instruction is too slow, students are apt to daydream or fall asleep; if too fast, stress levels skyrocket and actual learning decreases. In this section, we examine curriculum pacing and related issues.

The race to cover all the material from the textbooks and from the state assessment test can be maddening. Even if it were possible, covering all of this information isn't always an effective plan in the students' interest. Research has shown that if all the content in curriculum standards were actually taught

---

[2] Web site examples include www.naturalreaders.com and www.readplease.com. Commercial programs include Kurzweil and PDFaloud.

thoroughly, school years would need to be about 70 percent longer (Marzano, 2008). Marzano suggests that schools trim the content and cluster skills into no more than 15 critical learning goals for each grade level content area.

Curriculum committees, therefore, must identify which learning goals are essential for students to learn and which are nice to be familiar with but will not be essential to the student 10 years from now (Wiggins & McTighe, 2005). When curriculum committees rank goals by priority, teachers can then allocate appropriate amounts of instructional time to these goals. Some students seem to get things the very first time material is presented and can spend more time on lower-priority goals. Other students will need a lesson many times and in many ways in order to learn. Even though all students need full access to the general education curriculum, some items must realistically take a back seat to more critical skills.

A lesson's pace is critical to its effectiveness. Brain research shows that we can only hold a limited amount of information in working memory before we start losing pieces or mixing it up. The brain needs brief "rests" to allow neurotransmitters to restore its ability to carry messages and prevent overloading (Willis, 2006). With this in mind, think about pacing as teaching in "sound bites." Teachers present and model the information; then, before a glazed-over look sets in among the students, pace is completely changed to allow students to actively process the information (see Figure 6.3).

There is no research that tells a teacher exactly how long a lesson "sound bite" should be since many variables factor into the equation, such as a student's age, his or her emotional state, teacher enthusiasm, interest level of the material, prior knowledge, and timing of the lesson (i.e., if it is immediately before lunch or dismissal). That being said, there is research that indicates most children can focus for the number of minutes

Cluster skills and content into no more than 15 critical learning goals to make the curriculum more manageable.

The brain needs brief "rests" to restore its ability to carry messages and prevent overloading.

that matches their age plus two (Jensen, 1995). I have heard many kindergarten teachers echo this sentiment, saying, "That's right. If I can't say it in less than seven minutes, I'm toast." Good pacing is just as important in high school and at the university level as it is in preschool.

For our purposes, we will use this formula as a rule of thumb and say that a well-paced lesson looks like this:

1. Engage and focus students on the most important ideas in the lesson.
2. Model and present for no longer than students' average age plus two (shorter if the concept is complex or if there is a more logical place to pause).
3. Actively involve students in teacher-guided practice.
4. Let students first practice with support and then practice independently.
5. Summarize the lesson and give a preview of coming attractions (i.e., the next lesson or the next part of a lesson).

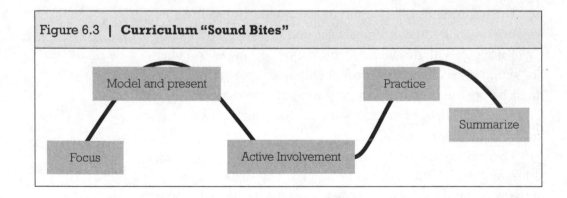

Figure 6.3 | **Curriculum "Sound Bites"**

Lesson pace must be lively with active and passive parts frequently shifting.

This cycle does not mean that, after students have practiced for a few minutes, teachers cannot summarize and start again with part two of the lesson. It just means that the pace must be lively with active and passive parts frequently shifting. The key is to remember that 30-minute lectures are not as effective as a lecture interspersed with dynamic processing.

In his interview on identifying characteristics of a good teacher, Barak Rosenshine stated,

> *We have found that the most effective teachers, those teachers whose classes made the highest yearly gain, provided a good deal of instructional support for the students. They provided this support by teaching new material in manageable amounts, modeling, guiding student practice, helping students when they made errors, and providing for sufficient practice and review. Many of these teachers also went on to experiential, hands-on activities, but they always did the experiential activities after, not before, the basic material was learned. (Clowes, 2002)*

Alternating teacher talk with student talk and reflection time significantly improves student comprehension and retention of material (Bonwell & Eison, 1991). This allows students to articulate their understanding of the material while reflection time improves memory and provides opportunities to clarify misconceptions. There are many ways to use the "pause button" during a lesson. Here is one example.

Pausing for reflection improves student comprehension, retention of material, and note-taking skills.

Mrs. Love introduces a science lesson by having partners use separate sticky notes to list each fact they already know about cells. Students have two minutes to do this. This pause provides a quick pre-assessment and focuses student attention on the day's lesson. Mrs. Love then tells students to place a check mark on each sticky note that includes a fact she talks about in class. She also provides a list of vocabulary words and concepts to listen for as well as a rough outline to use as a scaffold for note taking.

After eight minutes of teaching the structure and function of the cell wall, Mrs. Love says, "Turn and talk to your partner about the three most important things I've said about cell walls. You have two and a half minutes to do this and to expand your notes." Students share and revamp their notes as they compare ideas during this pause. Mrs. Love walks around the room and checks for misunderstandings or missed points. She then repeats this pattern—eight minutes of lecture followed by the "turn-and-talk" strategy—before giving independent assignments or small-group instruction opportunities.

Regardless of which pacing strategies are used, effective lessons begin by focusing students on the most important aspects of the material and take every opportunity to refocus students throughout the lesson.

Focusing Strategies

Teachers often say, "These kids just don't pay attention." The truth, however, is that students *do* pay attention. Unfortunately, the problem is that they may pay an inordinate amount of attention to their friends, their clothes, or the gum beneath their desks. The material that teachers want students to focus on is not necessarily grabbing their attention.

Once students feel safe, welcome, and engaged, their brains are free to focus on the salient points of a lesson.

Research shows that the brain sorts information according to a hierarchy of needs: the need to be safe and included, the need to be engaged by novel and enjoyable activities, and the need to achieve by problem solving (Willis, 2007). If a lesson does not address these needs early on, it promises to be an uphill battle. Once students feel safe, welcome, and engaged, their brains are free to focus on salient points and block out irrelevant ones. This, then, is the million-dollar question: What is and is not important in the mind of a student?

Previewing techniques

Previewing strategies decrease frustration and increase attention and receptivity by helping students sort through new information.

The human brain loves patterns. If new information doesn't fit into patterns of prior knowledge, it is often judged to be unimportant and discarded. Recognizing this, teachers need to show how new information connects to existing patterns that students are familiar with and interested in. Previewing strategies is one method to decrease frustration and increase attention and receptivity by helping students identify what is most important (Willis, 2007). In order to improve student focus, provide previews of coming attractions in the following ways:

- Post an attention-getting "essential question" in the classroom to get students thinking and talking about the topic. For example, "How would your life be different if we couldn't measure things?" Using this question as a launching pad, students begin to talk about how measurement affects their lives (i.e., they make connections between the new material and their prior knowledge).

- Post a classroom agenda that lists goals and topics so students can see what is coming down the pike. This also helps transitions go more smoothly.

- Start the class with a fun review activity, such as the 20-Second Talk. This activity serves as a lively review of recently studied material and helps students make new connections by articulating what they already know. The 20-Second Talk can also be used as a refocusing strategy in the middle of a lesson when students are tired and need a five-minute change of pace.

- Introduce a lesson by telling students what the final project will be and explaining how paying careful attention during the lessons can help them achieve success. For example, a physics teacher tells students that, within two weeks, they will be asked to build a paper airplane designed to fly farther and faster than anyone else's plane in the class. Students are given the critical principles and vocabulary that must be included in their final report, and they are told that they will have to defend the reasoning behind their designs. The authentic assessment can be taken one step further by having local experts (e.g., engineers from a local Air Force base) come to the classroom and judge the final reports and demonstrations. This definitely ups the ante. The teacher then explains that careful note taking during the following two weeks will provide them with all the information they need to do a great job. Students are much more likely to focus on a lesson if they recognize an objective that means something to them personally.

- Use music, games, and video clips to creatively grab students' attention. Be careful about what you select, though. If you cannot make a clear connection to your point, you may be introducing a distraction rather than enhancing comprehension.

ACTIVITY:	20-Second Talk
PURPOSE:	to review recently learned material to make connections to prior knowledge
MATERIALS:	none
GROUP SIZE:	students work with partners
TIME:	5 minutes

PROCEDURE:

Pair up students and tell them that they will discuss three different topics. Announce the first topic, and have Partner A tell Partner B everything he or she can remember about the topic in 20 seconds. After 20 seconds, say "Switch." At this point, Partner B takes over and adds a few points. Say, "Switch again," and have Partner A either add more information or summarize the main points. Use this same procedure for the other two topics. Walk among the pairs to get a feel for what students know so you can correct misunderstandings and clarify points during the lesson.

Note taking

When done well, note taking facilitates the synthesis and application of new knowledge.

Research shows that taking and reviewing notes helps students recall important information and score higher on tests. If done well, note taking also facilitates the synthesis and application of new knowledge (DeZure, Kaplan, & Deerman, 2001). Teaching students to take notes and use them efficiently is one of the best ways to help students focus on and process new information.

A good rule of thumb for showing videos in class is to never show more than a four- to seven-minute clip that makes the point you are trying to emphasize. The idea is to elaborate upon or illustrate an important concept, not to overwhelm students with distracting information. For example, if you are reading *To Kill a Mockingbird*, compare the climax of the book with the climax of the movie.

Nearly all teachers in classes above 4th grade expect students to take notes. Unfortunately, many districts don't systematically teach note taking as a skill across all grades and subjects. Instruction in effective note taking can start as early as kindergarten, and it should be refined and expanded each subsequent year.[3]

Note taking is more than simply copying facts. I have seen teachers write notes on the board in an effort to help students "get it right." It is a good idea to write on the board or supply a handout for very complex information like math formulas or diagrams, but real note taking involves actively extracting critical information and independently explaining core ideas and details (Hayes-Jacobs, 2006).

> Real note taking involves actively extracting critical information and independently explaining core ideas and details.

Heidi Hayes-Jacobs suggests that 3rd through 5th grade students use note cards for note taking. Students make entries for important facts as they learn, and they then organize their cards into categories. Organizing the cards helps them sort information that is important enough to be included from information that is more trivial. A focus on main ideas is essential to deep understanding. Middle school students should have regular practice

---

[3] A great resource that provides a wide variety of graphic organizers and ideas to guide students in note taking is a software program called *Inspiration* (*Kidspiration* for younger students). Another resource is a book called *Using Technology with Classroom Instruction That Works* (Pitler, Hubbell, Kuhn, & Malenoski, 2007).

with quick note taking and word elimination.[4] Timed practices, followed by note comparison among classmates, help students enhance their skills without omitting important items.

⚙ **HOW TO . . .** *make note taking work*

- Provide short pauses of silence while students are taking notes, unless your students' note-taking skills are automatic. Many students have no trouble listening or writing, but doing both at the same time can be problematic.
- Have students use their notes at the beginning of each class to review with a partner. This not only prepares them for new information, but it also reinforces the point that notes can be used as an effective study tool. This comes as a surprise to many students.
- Allow students to use their notes on some quizzes. This is a huge motivation to take thorough notes, and it reinforces the idea of using—not just taking—notes. Have students condense their notes to one index card for use during the test. This forces another review of notes as students select key facts for their cards.
- Teach in "sound bites" and pause so students can think about important points and compare information with partners before writing their own notes. Articulating what they just learned is a powerful memory boost, and it helps learners who have weak auditory processing systems or who have a tendency to "zone out."

Chunking Methods

When material comes in meaningful units (chunks), the brain can process more information because it recognizes patterns (Wolfe, 2001). As a demonstration, look at the following letters for eight seconds and then, on a separate sheet of paper, write them in the exact order (with correct spacing) on another paper. Don't look back to refresh your memory.

---

[4] Word elimination is an exercise where students look at an original passage or their own notes and distill the information down to the most critical ideas. This is done by deleting words that are not essential to what is being studied or researched. To teach this skill, the teacher generally identifies categories to be elaborated on or questions to be answered.

WER SVPO NT UES

How did you do? Most people have a hard time remembering a sequence that long because the letters do not form familiar words or create a recognized pattern. However, if we move the spaces and rearrange the letters into a familiar pattern, you will probably be able to do the exercise easily. Let's try again. Look at the letters below for eight seconds and then write what you remember on a separate piece of paper.

WE RSVP ON TUES

You probably did better, even though the same letters (in the same order) and the same number of spaces were involved. Why is this so? In the second group, the letters meant something to you. In the same way, if students are given a method to navigate the deluge of information that flies at them daily, they will be better prepared to handle even the most demanding workload. Chunking is a wonderful tool teachers use to help students learn more in a finite amount of time.

When material comes in meaningful units, the brain can process more information because it recognizes patterns.

Using more than one learning system also helps students learn more easily and thoroughly. Some teachers might balk at this and say, "I don't have time to teach it *one* way. Teaching with visuals, music, charts, and activities is great, but it takes too much time." What teachers really need to ask themselves is: Do I want to teach material carefully and deeply once, or do I want to keep reteaching it whenever students give me a blank stare? It is going to be a slow process either way, but in-depth teaching is less frustrating for the student. Three great ways of chunking material to increase comprehension and aid retention are graphic organizers, concrete and representational tools, and authentic learning.

Graphic organizers

Research suggests that graphic organizers help students see relationships and visualize unknown concepts to draw better conclusions (Hyerle, 1996). Research also shows that students who are taught to use graphic organizers before, during, and after reading have better comprehension and retention (Merkley & Jefferies, 2001). This strategy is helpful in every content area and at very grade level.

> Students who use graphic organizers before, during, and after reading have better comprehension and retention.

For example, an anticipation guide is a prereading organizer—used with small groups or individuals—that helps students think about important ideas in the text before they read about them, thus improving their comprehension. Teachers prepare anticipation guides by

1. Writing a series of four to six statements about major concepts of the text or possible misconceptions about those concepts.
2. Asking students to respond to the statements by agreeing or disagreeing with them before reading the text (this can be true/false, possible/impossible, etc.).
3. Having students read the text and list the page and paragraph numbers where information is found that confirms or negates their responses.

Figure 6.4 is a sample of an anticipation guide for reading a science article.

Concrete and representational tools

A veritable library of professional development modules on topics related to research-based practices is now available to educators at all levels. One such practice—the Concrete-Representational-Abstract (CRA) Instructional Approach—is appropriate from preschool through university levels (Access

Figure 6.4	**Sample Anticipation Guide Graphic Organizer**			
Agree or Disagree Before Reading	**Statement**	**Page #**	**Paragraph #**	**Agree or Disagree After Reading**
	Bottled water is healthier than tap water.			
	Labels on bottled water are required to have accurate information about the source of the water.			
	Much of the bottled water sold is not subject to FDA health regulations.			
	Leaving bottled water in a hot car often makes it potentially dangerous.			

concrete level. Teachers model abstract math concepts by using hands-on materials such as counters, blocks, coins, algebra tiles, virtual manipulatives, and measuring tapes. When students are comfortable with demonstrating their math understanding at this level, the teacher translates abstract concepts with two-dimensional representations such as drawings, pictures, and tally marks. If students can successfully verbalize their under-standing using pictures and drawings, then the teacher drops the two- and three-dimensional learning aids and uses only numbers and math symbols.

Research-based studies indicate that students who use concrete materials develop more precise and comprehensive mental representations, often show more motivation and on-task behavior, show better understanding of mathematical ideas, and more accurately apply these ideas to real-life situations (Harrison & Harrison, 1986).

The CRA instructional approach to math involves these steps:

1. Describe and model math concepts/skills with concrete objects (concrete level of understanding).
2. Provide students with multiple practice opportunities using concrete objects.
3. After students demonstrate mastery of a concept (five out of five for three consecutive days) using concrete objects, describe and model the concept with drawings or pictures that represent concrete objects (representational level of understanding).
4. Provide students with multiple practice opportunities where they draw their solutions or use pictures to solve problems.
5. After students demonstrate mastery (10 out of 10 for three consecutive days) with this approach, describe and model the concept with numbers and math symbols (abstract level of understanding).
6. Provide students with multiple opportunities to practice performing the skill using only numbers and symbols.
7. After students demonstrate mastery at the abstract level, ensure that they maintain this skill level by providing periodic practice opportunities.

As a teacher moves through a CRA sequence, numbers and abstract symbols should be used in conjunction with the concrete materials and representational drawings. This is especially important for students with special needs, since it promotes association of abstract symbols with their concrete and representational understandings. In higher grade levels, teachers typically start at the abstract level when they feel students already have mastery of the skill. If some students fail to demonstrate mastery, the teacher moves back to concrete and representational levels.[5]

Authentic learning

Simulations, games, and authentic projects have an enormous impact on memory and comprehension. A study by the Educational Testing Service (Wenglinsky, 1998) found that students who used computer simulations to learn mathematics concepts scored significantly higher on standardized tests than did students in classes where computers were used for "drill and practice." Authentic situations push students to organize their thinking and determine which factors are most important. They help students refine and communicate ideas and synthesize learning concepts and skills (Cherry, Ioannidou, Rader, Brand, & Repenning, 1999). Authentic situations also provide the most thorough approach to help students transfer and apply learning. There are many sophisticated ideas for authentic learning projects that involve debates, role playing, case studies, and computer simulations.

> Authentic situations help students organize their thinking and transfer and apply learning.

Real-life application of skills and concepts works well in every subject area. In fine and applied arts classes, authentic activities and assessments are a way of life. The music teacher never teaches notes and rhythms without intending to play the song. A coach doesn't teach players to pass or dribble the ball and then forget to play the game. Core subject areas need to have this same mentality—play the real game.

In science and physical education, teachers might ask, "What type of diet and exercise routine will help you increase

---

[5] Here are some other great resources for chunking math concepts: *Access Center. (n.d.)*. Algebraic concepts K–8 module. *Available: www.k8accesscenter.org/ training_resources/AlgebraicConceptsK-8.asp;* MathVIDS: Video Instructional Development Source. (n.d.). A Resource for Teaching Mathematics to Struggling Learners [home page]. Retrieved November 2, 2009, from http://www.coedu.usf.edu/ main/departments/sped/mathvids/index.html

your stamina?" In social studies, students can demonstrate ways to become an involved citizen by using problem-solving techniques to solve the slow lunch line problem in the cafeteria. Language arts teachers can have students compose books or videos to be used by younger grades.

Any time teachers make learning come alive by linking to what students think is important, motivation to learn goes up, along with academic achievement. I will, however, offer two notes of caution about authentic learning activities. First, do not let the projects become ends in themselves. I've seen students build models and dioramas while they miss the entire point of the lesson. Keep students focused on the *learning*—not just the *doing*. Second, make certain the amount of time your students spend doing the activity is worth the payoff in quality learning.

When I taught 3rd grade, my students struggled with making change and estimating a total price, so we set up a class store. The store was open every morning from 8:30 to 8:50. While the students were busy playing store, I greeted students, took lunch count, and filled out attendance slips. I also assessed a few students each morning for their ability to make change and estimate price. Everyone had fun taking their respective turns as clerk and shopper. Shoppers had to estimate the total cost of their purchase and the amount of change they should get while clerks performed exact computations. They saw themselves as real shoppers and worked hard at the role.

Practice and Rehearsal Strategies

Initial practice with a new skill should be a focused process using just a few examples.

Marzano, Pickering, and Pollock (2001) note that students don't generally achieve 80 percent mastery until they practice a skill at least 24 times. They state that the first four times a skill is practiced are the most critical and have the largest effect on learning. In the beginning, then, each practice should be a focused process with a limited number of examples, and each example should add a clear dimension of understanding to the skill. This can be done through modeling, think-alouds, and analogies to clarify the strategy and demonstrate when to use it. Guided practice with corrective feedback is also part of this phase. Increase speed only once students have a firm grip of the skill's "how" and "why." Speed and fluency allow the skill to become automatic, thus allowing the brain to focus on new learning.

Repeated reading

Repeated reading is a well-researched reading fluency intervention used for both normally developing and struggling readers (Linan-Thompson & Vaughn, 2007). For students to efficiently work on their reading rate, they must first be able to decode a passage with 95–100 percent accuracy (i.e., fewer than five mistakes in every 100 words). If reading accuracy is less than 95 percent, the text is probably too difficult for fluency practice. Figure 6.5 shows a strategy card that should be helpful in a Tier 1 or Tier 2 database.

Figure 6.5 | **Pyramid Card, Sample 4**

Teacher: Mary Jane Roberts

Appropriate for Grade Levels: 1–12

Date: December 2010

Intervention: Repeated Reading—This intervention is designed to increase reading fluency, comprehension, phrasing, fact recall, and enhance the study skill rereading for meaning. It can be used with a small group of below-average readers, including English language learners.

Materials: two or more copies of high-interest reading passages at the reader's independent or instructional level (e.g., textbook, newspaper, periodical, phrase flashcards, familiar or predictable texts)

Frequency and Duration: 15–20 minutes a day for at least six weeks

---

Figure 6.5 | Pyramid Card, Sample 4 (cont.)

Instructional Steps:

1. Calculate a baseline WCPM score based upon the median of three passages read orally. Graph the number of errors and WCPM. Errors include words misread, hesitations for more than five seconds, words skipped, and requests for help. 2. Allow students to select from a variety of materials to read, if possible. This helps maintain attention to the task.

3. Preteach unfamiliar vocabulary, give background knowledge about the passage, and model reading the story with expression. The amount of time changes with the age of the students (i.e., K–1 students listen for 45 seconds to 1 minute, 2nd to 4th grade students listen for 1–3 minutes, etc.) or until interest starts to diminish.

4. Have students read the passage aloud. Help students with words if they ask for help or hesitate for more than five seconds. Students should reread the passage silently or aloud (student's choice) several times (at least three). If students struggle after practicing, choral read together with them. Let them practice again and then reread the passage aloud. 5. Have each student reread the passage aloud as quickly and accurately as possible while you record errors and WCPM.

Variations:

1. Have students practice with partners. Each partner should read orally three times before reading for the teacher.

2. Have students choose a mood card and then read the passage to match the mood of the card they chose (e.g., sadly, humorously, angrily, lovingly). This strategy works better with older students.

3. Have young students use sight words in phrases, and have them practice using these phrase cards with each other.

4. Make recordings available on tape or CD so students can practice reading along during independent time. Students can also take these recordings home to practice.

Progress Monitoring: Once a week, conduct a one-minute review of oral reading using an unfamiliar passage. Graph the results.

Research Basis: Linan-Thompson, S., & Vaughn, S. (2007). *Research-based methods of reading instruction for English language learners, grades K–4.* Alexandria, VA: ASCD.

Teacher Comments: Use precounted passages to save time. Put the cumulative rate of words down the right side of the page after each line.

Incremental rehearsal

Incremental rehearsal can be used for elementary or secondary students who have low task completion (Burns, 2005). By interspersing easier problems with more difficult ones, students often complete more work due to the fact that frequent successes are built in as reinforcements throughout the exercise.

An example of incremental rehearsal might go like this. A student starts with two math flashcards: one with an unknown fact and one with a known fact (question or prompt on one side, answer on the other). The student practices until he responds correctly to each card within two seconds. He then adds a third card (with a known fact) to his practice pile. He gives the answer to each card until he can complete each of the three within two seconds. This pattern continues until he can complete 10 flashcards (nine known facts and the one new unknown fact) without error or waiting longer than two seconds for an answer. When this is possible, the student chooses a new "unknown card" and repeats the process.

> Students often complete more work when they have frequent successes built in to exercises as reinforcements.

Analogies

Making sense of information by comparing a new concept to something that is familiar deepens student understanding in any content area. Marzano and colleagues (2001) refer to the ability to see these similarities and differences as "the core of all learning" accomplished through teaching students to compare, classify, or create analogies.

Creating analogies involves seeing abstract similarities and differences. At first, students require a great deal of regular, guided conversation to see the relational reasoning between concepts that may have very little in common on the surface. Graphic organizers and visual representations can be used to enhance a student's ability to understand these similarities and differences. Here is an example of how you might use analogies to teach a science concept.

After learning about cell parts in science class, a 6th grade student had a homework project that involved the use of an analogy—he was supposed to make a model of a cell out of materials found at home. Cleverly, he wanted to buy a giant cookie and use various types of candy for the parts of the cell. The cookie represented the cytoplasm, and the student and his mother gathered objects that represented the functions of various organelles. The process of collecting and discussing how common household objects were like more abstract scientific concepts helped the student gain a better understanding of cell structure. Spurred on by an analogy, this process resulted in the student asking relevant questions and engaging in deep thinking.

Mom: What does the nucleus do?

Kenton: It controls the cell functions.

Mom: Okay, what do we have in this house that controls the functions of other things?

Kenton: The TV remote.

Mom: Perfect! That should go in the center of the cookie (in a baggie, though). Now, what do mitochondria do?

Kenton: They store and release energy, kind of like a battery.

By the end of the activity, Kenton had identified several items that clarified the somewhat abstract scientific concepts by making meaningful connections. Significant learning began at home, which could then be enhanced and expanded in the classroom. Authentic projects such as the one in this example should be used for homework very carefully. Many students don't have parents who are available to help deepen their thinking, or they don't have the materials and resources required. If the activity is worth doing, it should be done in class where the teacher can monitor and guide the thinking process. It is an all-too-common scenario when well-meaning parents complete their children's projects because the work is labor intensive with minimal serious learning involved.

Continuous Feedback

If you took beginner golf lessons and after each swing the only feedback your golf pro gave you was a letter grade from *A* to *F*, how helpful would that be? Helpful information cannot be reduced to a single letter or number; it has to be more specific. During the formative stages of learning, learners need clear information and guidance about what they are doing correctly and incorrectly. In the following sections, we will look at three strategies that positively influence both academic and behavioral growth when used appropriately: formative assessment, praise and criticism, and self-monitoring.

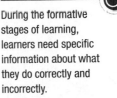

During the formative stages of learning, learners need specific information about what they do correctly and incorrectly.

Formative assessment and specific critiques

Marzano (2007) cites studies showing impressive effect sizes for schools that provide students with clear, timely, and specific feedback about their growth. Frequent formative assessments (assessments that provide multiple opportunities to "redo" as a result of feedback) meet this criterion and significantly improve student performance. The following is an example of how a formative approach to assessment—as opposed to a summative approach—might be used.

Mr. Smith returns a writing assignment to Richard with a *C–*. A common student response to this type of feedback is, "I'm not very good at writing." Richard then crumples up the paper and pitches it in the trash. End of problem.

Mrs. Jones returns the writing assignment to Richard, but, instead of a letter grade, she writes, "Your plot is an interesting one. This is going to be a great story. I also noticed that you are writing more sentences than you did last month. I want you to add two adjectives to each sentence. That will help your reader imagine the setting more clearly and understand your character better. See me if you need help on this. Draft two is due on Thursday." This is clear and specific feedback where the positive and corrective news is balanced. It helps teach Richard what it takes to improve, and it offers another chance to make those improvements before the final grade is recorded. Richard isn't overwhelmed with too many things to improve at once, but he is expected to improve his work.

Establishing a culture of redoing work—based on helpful feedback—to improve its quality is something lacking in most classrooms. Most teachers rely far too much on one-shot assignments. Students quickly learn that if they hand in garbage, then the worst consequence they face is a low grade. Who is truly motivated by the threat of a low grade? Students who generally get good grades. When a teacher says, "If you don't do better, you're going to get an *F*," students who typically get poor grades are likely to respond, "Knock yourself out. I'll probably get an *F* even if I do work harder." Even though teachers continually experience this reaction from struggling students, they still delude themselves into thinking that grades are an effective catalyst for a good work ethic. The truth is, how feedback is given to students speaks volumes about how a teacher views teaching and learning. Sometimes the viewpoint is "My job is to present the information and your job is to learn, and if that doesn't work out, then too bad for you. The grade is the grade." Other times, the viewpoint is "My job is to teach in as many ways as it takes to get you to learn. You may need more than one shot at it, and I will provide that." I know which teacher I want for my child.

Praise and criticism

To be powerful, praise must be clear and specific. Which statement would mean more to you: "You are a good educator" or "There are two things you do that I have always admired. One is the way you keep students engaged from the time you start a lesson until it's time to stop. The other is the way you use humor, without ever being funny at someone else's expense." Specificity makes all the difference.

Likewise, criticism must be clear and specific. When a teacher says, "If you would just pay attention, you wouldn't have such low grades," the student probably just loses confidence and feels bad. As an alternative, teachers should address this same lack of attention by saying, "I can see that it is hard for you to stay focused in class. Let me share a secret with you. People who don't find paying attention so hard have learned a few tricks to help themselves. One trick is called previewing skills. The second is a skill called 'pause and review in your head.' What do you think? If I help you, will you try these ideas and see if they work for you? I know you like art so let's start practicing these new skills in art class until you get comfortable with them."

HOW TO . . . *replace archaic grading systems with clear, specific feedback*

- Use clear and very specific feedback to increase understanding, especially in the early stages of learning.
- Balance the statements of strengths and weaknesses. Feedback is meant to provide encouragement as well as direction.
- Help students focus on two or three key skills to improve at a time. Attempting more will likely be overwhelming.
- Give students plenty of opportunities to edit and revise their work. Reworking the same assignment is often more beneficial than working on several different assignments.
- Turn negative feedback into goal statements. For example, "See if you can find and correct all nine punctuation errors in this paper."
- Recognize when students already know what it takes to improve and would benefit from brief feedback and guidance.
- Be consistent and honest in your feedback. Keep your scoring rubric the same for every student, and make sure that students understand the criteria before they start an assignment.

Though the comments address the same issue, the second approach will likely get a much more hopeful response from the student. Identifying only a few high-priority skills to focus on is important. My mother's advice holds true here (as in many aspects of life): Choose your battles carefully, or you will come out bruised and scarred.

Self-monitoring

Self-monitoring has been shown to be effective at reducing disruptive behaviors and increasing appropriate behaviors. It also increases academic performance, including on-task classroom performance and completion of homework assignments (Schunk, 1997). This is a strategy that is well worth the time it takes to implement.

Many students who become discouraged attribute their lack of success to a lack of intelligence or a poor relationship with the teacher. Serious trouble is indicated whenever success—or a lack thereof—is attributed to an outside, uncontrollable force. This results in an apparent lack of motivation, but it finds its roots in something far more serious: hopelessness and despair.

One of the most successful ways to teach students of the cause-and-effect relationship between effort and achievement is to have them self-score and chart their own progress (Hughes, Copeland, Agran, Wehmeyer, Rodi, & Presley, 2002). Using the progress monitoring strategies from Chapters 3 and 4 is a perfect way to start.

Students can analyze their own charts and decide if the selected strategies are working or not. If they are not, the teacher can involve the student in selecting a new strategy that he or she thinks will work better. This not only motivates students to beat their own best score, but it also instills them with the power to change things that are not working.

Summary

In this chapter, we looked at six powerful areas that make a significant difference in student achievement, when they are implemented with quality and consistency.

1. How safe and welcome do students feel in school?
2. How well are lessons paced to maximize attention and reflection?
3. How well are students kept focused on what's important?
4. How well is information chunked so students recognize patterns and make connections?
5. What kinds of practice and rehearsal strategies are in place to plan to increase retention?
6. What types of feedback are provided to increase motivation and achievement?

The job of every leader in a school district is to see that all teachers have the training and support necessary to help them intentionally address these areas in their daily lessons and routines. If every teacher in every class attends to the six research-based elements of instruction discussed in this chapter, the chances of having strong Tier 1 instruction is very high. When this happens, the numbers of students needing Tier 2 and Tier 3 support will decrease.

Building high-quality differentiated lessons that address the needs of both accelerated and at-risk students is exhausting and endless work. This job must be done by teams of professionals willing to share their combined experience and knowledge. The work must also be continually monitored, and the strategies must be adjusted when they don't match learners' needs.

Even the best instruction in the world can be rendered useless unless teachers genuinely care about kids and send subtle messages of support and reinforcement. This is the foundation upon which all other strategies rest. Each and every person in the district has a responsibility to see that no student becomes invisible and that no student becomes bored, overwhelmed, or rejected. When this threat is low and teachers use proven instructional strategies in the classroom, effective learning will take place.

7

What to Do When You Don't Know What to Do

In education, storms (of a seemingly infinite variety) just keep on coming as students struggle to acquire the skills that will enable them to become successful adults. As educators, we can choose to sit back and complain about these ongoing difficulties, or we can be proactive and learn new ways to overcome these challenges and get the job done. In the following conversation, Gerald, who is on the building leadership team, tries to help Morgan, an 8th grade science teacher, understand how the old Intervention Assistance Team (IAT) is going to change into the problem-solving model of RTI. This new model will enable them to more gracefully weather the educational storms that continue to come their way.

Morgan: So what was wrong with the old way we did IAT?

Gerald: The old way just wasn't giving us quick, effective help for kids. RTI is about action to achieve specific goals, not just labels. The RTI team should suggest concrete strategies we can do tomorrow, not just testing or accommodations we've already tried a dozen times.

Morgan: But even if they come up with powerful strategies, I don't have the time or training to help struggling kids who probably have disabilities. Specialists need to do that.

Gerald: RTI problem-solving meetings aren't just for students with disabilities. They're also for struggling general education kids who couldn't buy an IEP. Tell the truth, has there ever been a year when you didn't have kids who were struggling but weren't considered special ed?

Morgan: True, we all have those kids. All right, so the RTI teams will provide specific plans for any student at risk. How do we know when a student's problems are serious enough to refer?

Gerald: That's one big difference in our new system—we don't wait until a student is in deep trouble. RTI is about identifying problems as soon as they become apparent. The RTI team's job is to help you so you can help the kids.

What Makes the RTI Problem-Solving Process Different?

There are five aspects of the RTI model that may be a departure from the problem-solving model presently used in your district:

1. A referral process that includes a conference with an RTI coach to diagnose root causes of low performance or problem behavior
2. Action-only meeting guidelines
3. Parent and student preparation and involvement

4. The roles of parents, students, and experts in meetings
5. Data-driven follow-up meetings

By no means is this problem-solving model of RTI the only way to do business, but this approach has demonstrably paid huge dividends to every district and school in which it has been used. Before committing to the process, however, it's essential to first determine how well it fits your specific needs.

Many schools establish guidelines that require at least two steps before teachers can initiate a referral. Teachers need to document conversations with the student and his or her family about the problem, and they need to chart progress-monitoring data that illustrate the student's patterns of response (i.e., four data points below the goal line) for each of several Tier 1 interventions tried. Many schools require the involvement of an RTI team when the need for intervention could potentially move a student from one tier to another. Some schools take advantage of the RTI team's services to help with Tier 1 strategies, but most schools involve the team only when Tier 2 support is required.

> Teachers need to document problem-solving conversations and chart progress-monitoring results before they see an RTI coach.

Morgan: Two people I work with think that if their students are failing it's because the kids are just lazy or are special ed, and that's not the general ed teacher's problem.

Gerald: See, we're back to thinking that RTI is for special ed kids. Many students without disabilities fall behind as material gets harder, when a crisis strikes, during or after a move, or maybe after an extended absence. A short, extra boost of Tier 2 support could prevent failure if it is applied early enough. If the kid looks lazy, then we need to find out the cause of the problem, set a specific goal, and then actually do something about it. By the way, motivation is our job, too.

Morgan: You know it and I know it, but not everyone wants to admit that. Another issue is the mountain of paperwork required for a referral. That paperwork discourages even the most dedicated teachers. And then there's the long wait before the team even gets to the case.

Gerald: Our district leadership team agrees. Both of those issues were real weaknesses in our old system. With the new RTI model, a teacher will do little or no extra referral paperwork. They will only need information they already collected during Tier 1 instruction. This includes work samples, screening data, the progress monitoring chart showing results from each intervention, attendance and grades, parent contact information, and any background information that would be helpful.

Morgan: That's nothing more than good teachers should normally collect.

Gerald: Right. As for the timing problem, the intention is to train enough coaches so teachers never have to wait longer than a week for a referral conference, but that training might take a year or two. We will also use the expert pool to shorten the time between the referral and the actual meeting.

Morgan: How will the expert pool help shorten the time?

Gerald: The pool of resource people includes everyone in our school. That allows us to call on many people for RTI problem-solving meetings. If a student has a math problem and is having a hard time focusing, we call the math and attention experts. If the problem is reading and bullying, we call the experts on reading and bullying. We won't have to wait for the same group of five people to solve every type of problem.

Morgan: You know, that makes sense. People avoided serving on the IAT because of the time commitment involved with so many meetings. If this plan disperses the workload, that will be a huge step forward. Besides, our old IAT tended to suggest the same bunch of interventions without knowing if they were research-based. The experts should be able to deliver much better strategies. Couldn't teachers just go to these resource people and skip the whole referral thing?

Gerald: Absolutely. The goal here is not to have more meetings; it's to provide support to teachers as soon as they need it. If you can get new ideas by having a conversation in the hallway with the relevant expert, do it. If you need to involve a team and the family because the solution may require accessing more intense services and documentation, then go for the referral.

Morgan: Tell me more about student and family involvement in these meetings. That worries me. How can we talk freely if the parents and kids are sitting there?

Gerald: The old meeting style would pose a problem, but RTI problem-solving meetings have an entirely different tone. In fact, the number one rule is that talking about the problem is not allowed in the meeting. One hundred percent of the time is devoted to putting an action plan in place.

Assembling ad hoc teams of relevant experts from the expert pool helps to minimize wait time and maximize depth of expertise.

Morgan: How will we know what we are talking about if we can't mention the problem?

Gerald: We will all know what the problem is before we even come to the meeting. RTI coaches help teachers analyze the problem down to the root cause before the meeting.

In the past, time wasn't generally devoted to analysis of the problem before "solutions" were put in place. This approach is unfortunately similar to the carnival game "whack-a-mole"—as soon as you knock one problem down, two more pop up. Why did this happen? Too often, educators were not addressing the heart of the problem (the actual cause was, in many instances, still unknown). Teachers used Band-Aids when the problem really called for surgery.

In a successful RTI model, teachers use root causes of problems to set very specific DATA goals that guide the action plan (Searle, 2007). Having a DATA goal in place before the referral meeting allows several things to happen:

> Problems need to be analyzed—and causes need to be identified—before solutions can be put in place.

- Everyone comes prepared with three interventions that match the targeted problem, thereby shortening the meeting time.
- The number of problems under discussion is limited to two, thereby focusing energy on the most important issues.
- The interventions and accommodations are usually higher quality since people have time to prepare.
- Pre-agreed-upon goals allow the team to focus on the action plan, thus avoiding the defensive behaviors that often occur during problem-focused discussions.
- Accountability guides the team to determine whether the interventions are successful and efficient.

The RTI Coach

The RTI coach asks the pertinent questions that enable teachers to diagnose issues.

All of this begs the question "Who will help teachers identify the root cause of a particular problem so that clear goals can be set?" This responsibility falls to the RTI coach (see Figure 7.1). The coach doesn't perform the diagnosis, but he or she is trained to ask the pertinent questions that enable teachers to diagnose issues. This not only helps solve the problem under discussion, but it also builds capacity among the staff to recognize similar causes in the future. A successful RTI coach requires the right combination of personality and training.

RTI coaching requires good listening skills and the ability to ask tough questions while maintaining sensitivity to people's feelings. Good coaches are people who can

- Paraphrase, clarify, and briefly summarize important points.
- Ask hard questions without being offensive.
- Conduct a "five reasons" analysis.
- Distinguish root causes from symptoms.
- Write DATA goals.
- Suggest strategies for data collection that match the goal.
- Explain ways to measure and chart growth and interpret that data.

Individuals who make bad coaches

- Talk when they should listen.
- Try to solve people's problems for them.
- Refrain from asking difficult or uncomfortable questions.

When I first implemented this coaching process, I was the principal of a middle school with 1,000 students. We started with four building coaches—the counselor, the psychologist, the assistant principal, and me—and we practiced the skills among ourselves until we felt confident. Then we asked each of the grade-level teams to send one person to train with us. This person became that grade level's primary coach whenever an issue arose. This generally worked well for academic issues since the coaches had regular planning time with the people they served and they knew the students. However, this plan wasn't as efficient for cases where the student had consistent behavior problems.

When dealing with students who had relentless discipline problems, team coaches were often at a loss for appropriate interventions. Suggestions such as "Either she or I need to be shipped off to a class in Siberia" even had some appeal on particularly frustrating days. At that point, grade-level teams called on a coach from another team or on one of the building coaches for assistance. In addition to a fresh perspective and new ideas, this option also provided a resource person who was less emotionally involved with the students. This two-layered process was very helpful whenever the teams felt stuck.

The availability of coaches at two levels (grade and building) generally makes the referral process go more smoothly.

I subsequently became principal of an elementary school where I started the process in a similar way. I enlisted a core team of building coaches that consisted of the counselor, the psychologist, a reading specialist, and myself. Since this was a small elementary school with about 325 students, I thought the core team might be sufficient. After a few months, two teachers expressed interest in coaching training. They didn't know if they wanted to be coaches, but they were very interested in learning more about the process. Over the next four years, all but two teachers on staff were trained as coaches, and the faculty skill level for solving student problems was nothing short of remarkable. This full-training model was far superior to the model I used at the middle school for a number of reasons. First, with so many trained people, we never had a problem finding an available coach when we needed one. Second, coaching sessions were easier and shorter because everyone was intimately familiar with the procedure. Third, teachers regularly analyzed concerns informally because they had a new way to think about problems.

As a result of these experiences, I consistently recommend that schools schedule at least a one-day training on "five reasons" analysis, DATA goal setting, progress monitoring, and parent conversations. Districts that have used this whole-staff introduction find the entire RTI problem-solving process much easier to implement. This initial session also gives people a better chance to decide if they would like further training to become coaches. The more good coaches you have, the easier this process will be.

Figure 7.1 | **RTI Coach Job Description**	
What Do Coaches Do and Why?	
Purposes	**Duties**
• Assist in focusing and diagnosing problems. • Help the referring teachers see problems from a new perspective. • Provide support during implementation of the intervention process.	• Help gather and organize baseline data. • Diagnose using "five reasons" analysis. • Help establish the DATA goal. • Help select a progress monitoring instrument. • Help select and notify staff experts for the meeting. • Act as the parent contact.* • Act as the student's advocate.* • Touch base with teachers between meetings to see if the interventions are working. • Maintain a welcoming and safe environment during referral conferences. • Attend problem-solving meetings.††

* The coach acts as the parent contact or student advocate only when the relationship between the classroom teacher and the parent or student is not healthy enough to maintain the safe and welcoming atmosphere required for a productive meeting.
†† The coach generally does not have time in his or her schedule to attend problem-solving meetings and perform the diagnostic work required for referrals. I recommend not including them in the prescriptive part of the process. If you have many coaches, however, the time factor may not be a problem.

Getting Started

In the middle school, where our staff developed this model, the small group of four building coaches met weekly to teach one another more about coaching. We eventually developed the following four steps to guide the referral process and the procedure for creating an expert pool of resource people.

Distinguish causes from symptoms

Each month, the team selected one symptom of student behavior and one academic problem to work on. Each of us did background reading and came prepared to develop a list of potential causes for both problems as well as research-based solutions that were proven effective. At times, we invited people who had special training to assist us. For example, when we were working on reading problems, we asked two Title I reading teachers from the elementary school to join us.

Consider the following symptom: A student constantly daydreams in class. Think of and list six causes for this symptom. Make certain that you only list causes that are within your circle of influence. Don't list causes such as "poor family support" or "low IQ" because those things are beyond your control. Even though they are important issues, dwelling on things you can do nothing about is counterproductive. Compare your list with these common causes for daydreaming:

- The work is too hard or too easy.
- The student has run out of energy and needs a mental break.
- The student cannot connect this information to prior knowledge.
- The student is confused about the requirements and doesn't ask for help.

> Coaches need to recognize the difference between a root cause and a symptom.

- The student feels disconnected from the teacher, his or her peers, or the material.
- The student is not an auditory learner, and the teacher only lectures in class.

If a teacher doesn't look past student behavior to its underlying reason, the likelihood of selecting an appropriate intervention is low.

A good coach will always consider a number of possible causes for any student problem. If a teacher doesn't look past student behavior to its underlying reason, the likelihood of selecting an appropriate intervention is low. For example, to solve our sample problem and eliminate daydreaming, we wouldn't want to lower the level of material for a bored student, nor would we want to increase lesson pace for a student who can't link the material to his or her prior knowledge. Coaches help teachers conduct a successful root-cause analysis for each student, but, in order to do this, both coach and teacher need to know a few things about the student before beginning. The second step, then, is a way to "cut to the chase" and identify strengths and concerns.

Identify strengths and concerns

Our group experimented with many ways to collect baseline information. Ultimately, we decided that teachers did not need more paperwork, nor did they need to wait for countless tests to be given before getting help. In our system, coaches asked: What skills and behaviors are you worried about? What strengths and interests does this student have in place?

Coaches learned to summarize the teacher's concerns on a Strengths and Concerns Form. Concerns directly related to the state's academic standards were written on the academic side of the form, and behavior concerns were listed on the right. It is important to remember that "behavior concerns" include more than discipline problems. This category includes all nonacademic concerns, including fear of making mistakes, lack of class participation, incomplete assignments, and missed homework assignments. Separating academic from behavioral concerns helps the team balance its intervention approach. Sometimes teachers fail to recognize that the root cause of poor behavior is a fear of academic failure. Likewise, the reverse can also be true—poor behavior may interfere with academic growth. This is why our team always chose two problems on which to focus at the first RTI coaching session: one academic and one behavioral.

Our coaches learned to help teachers choose a high-leverage concern to start with. Where you start can often impact the gains that a student makes. For example, a student cannot comprehend what he reads, and he also struggles with spelling, grammar, sentence structure, and computation fluency. Of all the choices, a focus on reading skills would have the highest impact since comprehension affects overall achievement more than the other concerns.

Once two high-impact issues have been selected, the teacher and coach should list the student's strengths. Thinking about and listing student strengths often results in a long pause as the teacher switches mental gears. To facilitate this process, our team designed a sample listing of strengths (see Figure 7.2) in several categories, including communication, reading, math, memory, and interests. This sample helped teachers focus and helped speed the referral process along.

Consider this scenario: a 7th grade student has 2nd grade reading comprehension problems (academic), and he refuses to do his work (behavioral). In this case, the coach first asks the teacher to list the student's reading strengths. Looking at the glass half empty, the teacher might be tempted to say, "Hardly any. He barely reads a thing." Looking at the glass half full, though, she might say, "He can sound out most two-syllable words. He can pick out the main idea if material is on his level or if someone reads the higher-level material aloud. His reading fluency is 85 words per minute at a 2nd grade level." Both the

> Choose two problems to focus on at RTI problem-solving meetings: one academic and one behavioral.

Figure 7.2 | Sample List of Student Strengths

Communication:
- asks questions
- sees relationships
- expresses feelings openly
- writes well
- draws well
- is a reflective thinker
- is a creative thinker

Reading:
- uses parts of book
- can blend sounds
- uses vowel rules to sound out words
- can identify sight words
- attends to punctuation when reading
- reads with fluency
- can separate important from unimportant
- visualizes as he reads
- links text to prior knowledge
- enjoys reading

Memory:
- recalls details seen
- recalls details applied
- recalls feelings
- can sequence ideas learned
- recalls after intense practice
- can link new ideas to old ones
- remembers the next day
- remembers a week later
- strong long-term memory
- visualizes to remember
- develops memory tricks

Social/Emotional:
- is organized
- does things step-by-step
- has high energy
- is excited about learning
- works well alone
- likes to solve problems
- believes in himself
- handles setbacks well
- works within deadlines
- likes competition
- sees many options and solutions
- works hard
- wants to succeed

Math:
- recognizes numerals
- knows one-to-one correspondence
- counts well
- understands place value
- understands regrouping
- understands equal values
- can visualize the problem
- understands math vocabulary
- can solve problems multiple ways
- can explain his reasoning

Interests & Talents:
- sports
- animals
- art
- music
- computers
- writing
- collections
- cars, bikes, etc.
- fashion

coach and teacher are responsible for steering the discussion toward this optimistic, productive line of thinking.

The coach then asks about work habits, since the student's refusal to do work is the key behavioral concern. Knowledge of student strengths, as well as information about interests, special talents, and strengths in other content areas, is helpful in order to identify an appropriate intervention. If the teacher does not have this kind of information, the RTI coach helps find someone who can assist the teacher in collecting it. As a result of this discussion, the coach completes a Strengths and Concerns Form, as shown in Figure 7.3.

Figure 7.3 | Strengths and Concerns Form

Academic Concerns:	**Behavioral Concerns:**
• has weak math computation	• seems bored by everything
• doesn't complete word problems	• has low energy
• doesn't comprehend when reading	• makes many careless errors
• has poor spelling	• often refuses to work
• doesn't write in complete sentences	• is passive in class
• has weak grammar skills	

Strengths to Build On:

- can decode two-syllable words
- reads 85 words per minute (2nd grade level)
- can identify main idea (2nd grade level)
- seldom breaks school rules
- works well with partners
- speaks Spanish at home
- seldom misses school
- likes football and soccer
- has strong visual associations
- knows math place values to thousands
- matches pictures of fractions with values

Conduct a "five reasons" analysis

The "five reasons" analysis is an adaptation of the "five whys" business strategy begun by Toyota. Asking "why?" five times generally reveals the root cause of (and, sometimes, the solution to) a problem. Our coaching team quickly found out that it is important for the questioner to recognize the difference between a symptom and a root cause, or else the process is severely compromised and weakened. In addition, while it typically takes five iterations of asking "why?" to arrive at a root cause, it can certainly require more. One of the most common mistakes new coaches make is stopping the process before they actually identify a significant root cause.

> Asking "why?" five times generally reveals the root cause of a problem.

The coach can start the "five reasons" analysis with either the academic or the behavioral issue. In practice, many coaches prefer to start with the behavioral issue, since the process seems to progress more smoothly when the most "annoying" issues are covered first. The objective is to help the teacher recognize underlying causes by asking some version of the question "Why is this happening?" Regardless of the actual phrasing, the answer must result in a reason behind the problem. Here are helpful rules for coaches to follow during this process:

1. Act as a sounding board, not the problem solver. Let the teacher unravel the problem while you guide the process. To do this, ask only "why-type" questions. Keep opinions to yourself unless the teacher is totally stuck. For example, if a teacher says, "Shelly will not do her homework," you should ask, "Why do you think she chooses not to do it?" Do not say, "Have you tried assigning her a homework buddy?" or "Do you think the work is too hard?" Such questions essentially plant solutions in the teacher's mind and do not invite him or her to analyze the situation.

2. Incorporate the most important words from the teacher's answer into your next question. This forces you to actively listen and keeps the conversation from diverting away from its original focus. If the teacher says, "Jasmine cannot pay attention in class," your next question should be "Why is she having trouble paying attention?" Even though you might want to know about note taking, for example, you shouldn't ask, "Does she have trouble taking notes in class?" It is best to see where the teacher will take the original thought. Make a note of clarifying questions to ask after the "five reasons" analysis, unless clarification is necessary in order to proceed.

3. Listen to the teacher's meaning as well as his or her words. Sometimes, it is helpful to paraphrase what you infer and incorporate this thought into the next question. If the teacher says, "I don't think Jean can learn phonics," you might paraphrase by asking, "Are you saying that even a reading specialist couldn't teach her phonics?" If the teacher agrees, then proceed with the next "why-type" question: "Why do you think Jean is incapable of learning phonics skills?" If, however, the teacher responds with "Maybe a specialist could do it, but I can't," then your follow-up question should be "What can a specialist do that you cannot?" This will help clarify if the teacher needs training or if the teacher thinks the student needs more help than is possible in a general education class.

4. Allow sufficient time for teachers to think about your questions and formulate a response. Many times, teachers just need additional time to think through a situation after they initially answer, "I don't know." If the teacher really doesn't know the answer to your question, then it is your responsibility to prompt him or her with three possibilities. Giving multiple choices keeps the ball in the teacher's court, but it also provides new options and a fresh perspective for thinking through potential causes. For example, you ask, "Why do you think Brenda struggles with solving math problems?" In response, the teacher says, "I have no idea, and don't ask me why. If I knew why, I would have it solved already." To guide the teacher to the next step, you should say, "Okay, let me suggest three common causes, and you tell me if any of these sound like a possibility to you: (1) Brenda cannot read the math problem, (2) Brenda doesn't see math patterns, or (3) Brenda cannot visualize the problem."

If the teacher says that none of these sound like possibilities, give a few more possibilities until something sounds right. If you are not a math expert and your list of possibilities is exhausted, you may need to call in a math expert to help you with the case.

Root causes must be within the coach's sphere of influence in order to do something about them.

The "five reasons" analysis is not an easy process, but it is probably one of the most powerful skills you will learn as an RTI coach. Asking these questions peels away the layers and cuts to the heart of nearly any problem, so the conversation may be a scary one for some people. During the analysis, be careful not to lay blame or talk in vague generalities. Remember: the bottom line always lands directly in the educator's lap—it has to or it won't be in your circle of influence to change. For example, you cannot change the fact that no one is at home to help practice math facts with the child, but you can give the student more practice at school.

I was once involved in a training session where groups were practicing the "five reasons" analysis with their own case studies. One of the principals motioned for me to come over, and he then whispered, "What if we figure out the problem is the teacher?" This is a common concern. My response is "It's always about us. Just because the teacher has a problem situation doesn't necessarily mean that he or she is a problem teacher. It means that he or she just hasn't found the right button to push to get a better result. The answer has to focus on something we *can* do but *aren't* doing."

If, during a "five reasons" analysis, you find yourself in a helpless place, then you are likely outside your sphere of influence. Revisit your questions and answers to see where you went wrong and ask a new question. For example, a teacher says, "Evan cannot stay in his seat" and you then ask, "Why doesn't he stay there?" The teacher responds, "I think he needs medication, but his parents refuse to take him to the doctor." At this point, if you ask anything about medication, the conversation will go nowhere. It will effectively be outside your sphere of influence. Redirect the interview and ask, "Other than possibly needing medication, what other reason might cause Evan to get out of his seat at the wrong time?" It is your job as the RTI coach to help teachers see beyond the cause and solution they have already considered.

It is clear that RTI coaches need to be skilled communicators. It is vital that the "five reasons" conversations be conducted without making teachers feel blamed or guilty. Teachers must always feel that the coach is on their side and that, together, they are constructively working toward a better solution. Consider the following example:

> Teachers must always feel that the coach is on their side and that, together, they are constructively working toward a better solution.

Carlos is failing science and social studies. He goes to Title I for Tier 2 supplemental reading support, but he does well in math. His science and social studies teachers bring his case to the RTI coach. The coach has already addressed Carlos's behavioral issue of not completing assignments. The first "five reasons" session addressed Carlos's unwillingness to ask for help when he needs it. When asked why he doesn't ask for help, Carlos said, "Making mistakes and asking questions makes you look like a loser in front of your friends." After the "five reasons" analysis, Carlos's teacher decided that the root cause of this problem was Carlos's perspective of making errors and not knowing answers. As a result, she asked the team to come up with ways to help Carlos see errors as opportunities to learn, not something to hide.

With the root cause of the behavioral problem addressed, the coach and teachers turn their attention to the academic issue of not responding accurately to questions asked orally or in writing. Figure 7.4 presents the sequence of questions and responses for this "five reasons" analysis.

In this scenario, the coach had to ask six "why-type" questions to arrive at what the teacher saw as a cause for Carlos's inaccurate responses. As mentioned before, one of the biggest mistakes coaches make is not going deep enough. If, after two questions, they think they have a new way of seeing the problem, new coaches often stop asking questions. I suggest continuing and going deeper, even if you think you have identified a good cause.

Figure 7.4 | Example "Five Reasons" Analysis Interview

Coach's Questions	Teacher's Responses	Coach's Clarifying or Paraphrasing Comments
1. Why do you think Carlos doesn't respond accurately in class?	I think he is just lazy. He doesn't pay attention during lectures, he seldom finishes his assignments, and his homework is never complete.	What does he do that makes you think he is lazy? (The coach chooses one issue and comes back to the others later, if needed.)
2. What causes Carlos to tune out during class?	He seems to think he can't do the work anyway, so why try?	
3. Why doesn't he think he can do the work?	He has a hard time with reading, writing, and even listening. He can do better than he does, but it is hard for him.	So you're saying he doesn't have the skills to be successful even when he tries? Let's take these skill problems one at a time.
4. Tell me why he struggles when he's reading in your classes?	He just doesn't get it even if someone reads things to him. I think he has a low IQ.	Since we cannot control IQ, we have to find another answer that we can influence.
5. Other than possibly low ability, why do you think Carlos struggles with even auditory comprehension?	His parents don't speak English, so they can't help him much, and the language thing could be a problem for him.	
6. Why would Carlos's bilingual ability cause a problem in science or in social studies?	It wouldn't, unless he is struggling with English vocabulary more than we think he is. I suppose that could be an issue for reading, writing, and listening. I think that might be part of it, especially if we help teach Carlos to ask for help when he needs it.	So you think if we work on his vocabulary skills in science and social studies, his reading, writing, and listening will improve? Great. Let's use those two strategies. Vocabulary development and teaching Carlos to ask for help will be the *D* part of our DATA goal.

The second most common mistake that new coaches succumb to is identifying a "solution" before a root cause is identified. For many teachers who are used to solving innumerable problems throughout a typical day, it is hard to switch gears and talk about causes.

The third pitfall coaches must learn to avoid is going outside their sphere of influence. Common statements that steer the conversation into this realm include "She has family problems," "There are physical or mental disabilities," "There is no support or discipline at home," "Last year's teacher was a problem," "He moves a lot," and "She needs medication or other medical assistance." If any of these issues come up during the "five reasons" analysis, good coaches make a note and follow up with the principal, counselor, or a community agency. They do not pursue the topic with the teacher during the "five reasons" analysis since it is not directly within their control. The coach should maintain focus on issues and causes that can be influenced immediately in the classroom or by a member of the school's expert pool.

Three common coaching pitfalls: not asking enough questions to get at a root cause, identifying a solution before the cause is determined, and going outside your sphere of influence.

HOW . . . *to maintain focus as you conduct a "five reasons" analysis*

Ask yourself the following questions:

- Is the issue within my circle of influence? (i.e., Is it something I can change?)
- Is the teacher's response too general or too specific?
- Are we jumping to solutions before the root cause has been identified?
- Is my next question based on the key concept just mentioned by the teacher?
- Does my question ask for clarification or analysis?

Set a DATA goal

The secret to short, productive meetings is to ensure that each team member understands the focus in advance and comes prepared. In order to come prepared, people must receive a DATA goal several days before the RTI problem-solving meeting.

DATA goals are clear measurable targets used to guide the team's actions. Introduced in Chapter 4, DATA is an acronym for

D—Different approaches by staff (i.e., new strategies and procedures)

A—new **A**chievement level expected from students

T—amount of **T**ime until the goal can be achieved

A—**A**ssessment evidence that indicates if the goal has been accomplished

If we continue with Carlos's case, his science and social studies teachers, along with the RTI coach, would complete a DATA goal that might resemble this:

D – If we teach Carlos new methods to build his vocabulary in science and social studies and help him feel comfortable enough to voluntarily ask for clarification when he needs it,

A – his success in understanding science and social studies concepts will increase.

T – six weeks

A – Success will be documented by an increase in correctly identified vocabulary at a rate of two additional words per week. A vocabulary progress-monitoring assessment will be used to measure this. If Carlos requests assistance on at least 50 percent of the assignments he struggles with, we will judge this as adequate success on that issue.

When setting a DATA goal, the *D* should not be one specific strategy. It should be a new skill taught in a way that has not already been tried. DATA goals generally use the sentence starter *If we teach (the student) to (target behavior). . . .* For example, if the "five reasons" analysis determined that a student cannot separate key ideas from details, you might write a statement

The *D* should not be one specific strategy.

that begins, "If we teach Lance to separate main ideas from details. . . ." Statements such as "The teacher should use a split-page organizer to help Lance separate main ideas from details" is too limiting because it names one specific strategy. At this stage, it is better to be more general so the RTI team can suggest multiple ways a teacher might approach the core problem.

The *A* is also relatively simple to write—it is just a retooling of the teacher's original concern. In Lance's case, the teacher's original concern was that Lance daydreams when he should be taking notes, and the "five reasons" analysis concluded that this occurs because Lance can't distinguish between what is important and what is not. Lance's DATA goal looks like this:

The *A* restates the teacher's original concern.

D – *If we teach Lance to separate main ideas from details,*

A – *he will be able to reduce his daydreaming and take good notes in class.*

Unlike the *D* and *A* of the DATA goal, the *T* must be very specific. This is the group's best estimate of how long it will take for the plan to show growth. It is usually better to set a modest growth target and check for progress within six weeks than to let an untested plan progress for a long time.

The *T* should be a modest timeframe, generally not longer than six weeks.

The last *A* must also be very specific. This describes how progress will be assessed toward a specific benchmark. In order to determine a reasonable benchmark, teachers must know the student's ability level before an intervention begins. Consider Carlos's benchmark goal. Asking for assistance 50 percent of the time may initially sound like a weak goal, but if he currently never asks for help, it is actually a very ambitious goal. Make certain that the assessments selected meet the following criteria:

The last *A* must be a very specific measurement toward a defined benchmark.

- They are sensitive to small changes in growth.
- They are easy to collect.
- They measure exactly what you want to see changed.

Measurement of progress toward a goal must also be very precise. Statements such as "measured through observation" simply don't cut it. If you cannot graph it, it isn't specific enough. Examples of effective measurements include these:

- Lance will be able to separate main ideas from details 60 percent of the time on relevant assignments.
- Pedro's notes will contain at least 60 percent of the key ideas discussed in class.
- Jerry's words per minute read correctly will increase from 32 to 38.
- Markay's classroom disruptions will decrease from an average of seven to three times per class, and her time on task will increase from 60 percent to 75 percent.

DATA goals should make it easy for team members to know what type of intervention ideas to bring to the problem-solving meeting. With a fully developed DATA goal, the team will be able to accurately judge the success and effectiveness of an RTI plan based on specific data collected by the teacher, student, and parents.

⚙ **HOW TO . . .** *proceed without a problem-solving meeting*

Not all referral conferences result in a problem-solving meeting. If, after the referral conference, a teacher feels as though he or she knows what to do next, there is no need to schedule a meeting. This happens about one-third of the time. Remember to keep the paperwork in case things don't work out as expected.

Setting Up the Problem-Solving Meeting

After the coach helps the teacher complete the strengths and concerns interview, conducts the "five reasons" analysis, and helps set the DATA goal, the logistics for the problem-solving meeting must be determined. This involves the following decisions:

- Who will be invited to attend the meeting?
- Who will call the parents to explain the referral results and meeting guidelines?
- Who will prepare the student for the upcoming meeting?
- Who will make the follow-up courtesy call?

The problem-solving meeting is a collaborative effort wherein the faculty, family, and student jointly develop a specific action plan that supports and accelerates the student's academic and behavioral growth.

Select team members and clarify roles and expectations

The size and makeup of the team for the problem-solving meeting will vary with each case. Some schools maintain one or two core members in the interest of consistency and add experts as needed. Although there are advantages to having consistent and well-trained members on the team, using *only* core members limits expertise and growth opportunities for others. It also wears out the core team and limits the number of students who can be served. A professional development goal, therefore, should be to increase the number of staff available and able to serve as "problem-solving experts" for a wide variety of cases. Five to seven people is generally a good size for the team; there is nothing more unnerving for a parent or student than walking into a room full of educators and feeling outnumbered.

A typical problem-solving team generally includes

- An administrator to allocate resources and enforce rules.
- The referring teacher or teachers. (If several teachers make the referral, the team generally selects one or two representatives.)
- The parent(s) or guardian(s).

- The student.
- Two resource people who have expertise relevant to the type of problem and intervention under consideration (e.g., content experts, social workers, therapists, nurse, behavior experts).

As previously mentioned, everyone should come to the meeting prepared with three interventions that will help the student reach the established DATA goal: one for parents to do at home, one for staff to implement at school, and one for the student to use at home or school. All members (including the student and parents) should be an active part of the team and focus on identifying solutions.

How many times have you had (or heard) a conversation such as this, after a student conference?

Dana:　How did your conference go?

Kay:　I'm considering going home to kick the couch. Does that answer your question?

Dana:　Uh oh, that's not like you. Is your dad still in the hospital?

Kay:　Yes, and if that isn't enough, my oldest daughter is dating Denny Dimwit, my husband's company is talking about layoffs, and I have a hangnail. My stress level is absolutely through the roof, and the teacher says Sonya is getting an *F* because she isn't motivated and doesn't do her homework. Homework! Are you kidding me? My life is crumbling around me and she wants me to do battle over homework!

Dana:　I know you've had a lot on your plate over the past few months. I'm sure the teacher has no idea what you are up against right now. She's probably frustrated because she doesn't know what to do, either.

Kay: That's probably true, but she has to understand that I am at a point with Sonya where I have to pick my battles, and homework is not the hill I want to die on. I know her school has special ed classes and after-school help available, but Sonya balks at any help that singles her out. The teacher thinks Sonya is unmotivated, but I really think Sonya's been on the edge of struggling for such a long time that she really doesn't understand the material now that it's getting harder. I wish there were other options for helping her.

More options for helping students is exactly what teachers and parents need. The RTI problem-solving system does just that. Parents who have experienced a variety of problem-solving formats are consistently amazed and delighted at how well the RTI process meets their families' needs. This process is especially effective because

- Communication between the teacher and the home is consistent and proactive.
- The focus is always on specifically what to do instead of what is wrong.
- No member of the problem-solving team dictates actions to the rest of the team. The parent doesn't tell the teacher how to run the classroom, and the teacher doesn't tell the parent how to run his or her home. Each person selects the best-suited strategy from a list of options generated by the team for reaching the student's two targeted goals.
- Parents' opinions and insights are solicited and respected, and their involvement makes them part of the team, not a victim of it.

The RTI problem-solving process focuses on what to do instead of what is wrong.

Make the parent call

Typically, about a week before the meeting, the teacher makes a call to the referred student's parent. In this phone conversation, the teacher clearly spells out the DATA goal being suggested for the student, as well as who will attend, where the meeting will be held, what the meeting guidelines will be, and what the parent can do to prepare for the meeting. The goal of this call is to create and maintain positive and open communication with the family as the school and home work together to support the child.

HOW TO . . . *conduct the parent call*

1. Describe the purpose of the meeting, as summarized by the DATA goals.
2. Gather data about the student's strengths and concerns from the parent's viewpoint.
3. Explain who will be asked to serve on the team and why.
4. Schedule the meeting (date, time, and place).
5. Go over the "rules of the road" that will guide the meeting.
6. Explain everyone's assignment (i.e., three interventions that will help the student meet his or her DATA goal).
7. Mention the courtesy call, to be made within 48 hours, that will answer any questions or help them come up with interventions.

Here is how a call might sound after the teacher finishes the referral conference with the coach about Sonya:

Teacher: Hello, Mrs. Tullis, this is Amanda Zornes, Sonya's English teacher.

Mother: Hi, Miss Zornes. Did you have the conference with the coach?

Teacher: Yes, and I think we have come up with some possibilities. One thought we had was that Sonya might not be processing information in class as quickly as it comes at her. We think she needs little mental rehearsals within the class period.

Mother: You would be willing to change your whole class to accommodate Sonya?

Teacher: Accommodating Sonya is my job, but it isn't as one-sided as it sounds. We have been studying brain research, and we are seeing that this is a good practice to use with all kids. Sonya just needs it more than some others. Does that sound right to you?

Mother: Yes, it does. How will that help the homework problem? I'm still worried about that.

Teacher: If Sonya understands what is taught, the homework shouldn't take so long. We also think that her motivation is low because she doesn't see any improvement when she does work hard. We have created a second goal to address that issue. All of us, including you, need to help her see how she is improving as a result of the work she does. We need to find better ways to give feedback on her progress.

Mother: I'm not sure feedback is going to help, but let's try. How will we do that?

Teacher: Well, now that the coach and I have identified the possible source of the problem, we will all meet with the RTI team. They will help us generate a list of ways to make these things happen.

Mother: I can't wait to see this meeting. Who are the RTI people?

Teacher: The team will include you, Sonya, me, and two teachers who are experts in the areas with which Sonya needs help: lesson pacing and motivation

When working on one student's case, it is helpful to think of other students who might also benefit from the same intervention.

Mother: OK, when is this meeting scheduled?

Teacher: We typically meet on Tuesday mornings from 8:00 to 8:20, but I know you're at work from 7:30 until 2:00. We can meet a week from Thursday at 3:30 in the library if that's okay.

Mother: That will be fine. Just have Sonya meet me there rather than get on the bus.

Teacher: Let me explain the "rules of the road" for our meetings. There are just two big ones. First, there will be no discussion of the problems in the meeting. We only discuss how to reach the two goals that we agreed to focus on. That will help Sonya feel safe in the meeting. If anyone forgets this rule, please feel free to stop them from talking about a problem. If you forget, we will do the same for you. Second, everyone who comes to the meeting is part of the team, and everyone—including you and Sonya—needs to bring three ideas for helping Sonya meet her goals. One of your ideas should address how you think the teachers can reach Sonya better, one should address how you can help Sonya at home with the motivation goal, and one should be something you think Sonya can do to help herself.

Mother: I don't know that I can come up with three ideas. I'm not a teacher.

Teacher: Don't worry. We're not looking for teaching ideas from you. We want ways to help Sonya from a parent's point of view. I have a list of things other parents have suggested to us, if you think that might help. Would you like a copy? Oh, and another staff member will make a courtesy call within 48 hours to see if you have any other questions or need help with ideas.

Mother: That sounds great. Yes, please send me the list. What if I can only come up with one thing?

Teacher: Then we'll take the one idea you have. Don't worry about that. We just want to make sure that we're listening to your ideas. I do have to tell you, though, that none of us is required to select another person's suggestions. They're just options we can choose from.

Prepare the student

The same basic checklist and guidelines used to prepare parents can also be applied to the student conference. This typically takes about 20 minutes. The person conducting the session needs to be someone with whom the student feels safe. When a discipline issue is involved, classroom teachers may not feel as though they can play the role of student advocate effectively. In these cases, find someone more neutral to fill the role.

The student advocate first explains the DATA goals in "student language." It may sound like "It seems that writing is really tough for you and you don't like to do it. Is that right?" If the student agrees, the advocate can try a modified "five reasons" approach to elicit the student's viewpoint. Often, students will reply with "I don't know" or just shrug. Be patient and wait for a possible response. If nothing comes forth, suggest a few of the reasons that developed from the "five reasons" analysis. If the student agrees with this assessment, then explain the meeting procedures and identify the team members. If the student disagrees, you may want to revisit and adjust the DATA goal to be a better fit. If the student has no buy-in, the best interventions in the world are doomed. The advocate has to let the student lend his or her voice to the process. Give and take on the part of both the student and the adults is a major component for making this process work efficiently.

There is one main difference between the parent call and the student conference. In the student conference, the advocate and student develop a list of possible interventions for each category (parent, teacher, student). The student then selects one strategy for each of these categories that he or she thinks will help achieve the goal.

I have gone through this process with kindergartners through high school seniors, and their reactions are very similar—a shrug—after they are asked, "What do you think your teacher could do to help you learn this more easily?" The advocate needs to go to this conference with ideas ready, but the student is the one who makes the final selection. This creates a sense of responsibility and ownership, and it also sends the message "This plan is not going to be done *to* you but *with* you."

With young kids, I often write their ideas on a card with accompanying pictures to help them remember what we talked about. Then, during the meeting, they are able to post their own ideas on the idea chart with everyone else's.

Conduct the action-only meeting

What distinguishes the action-only meeting is the guideline that absolutely prohibits any talk of problems the student is having. This might appear to just be a matter of semantics, but discussing the problem in the form of a goal completely changes the meeting's tone. The meeting should exclusively focus on the action that will close the gap for the identified academic and behavioral issues.

RTI problem-solving meetings are generally 20 minutes long. This might be a bit different from meetings you are currently used to, which could last anywhere from 45 minutes to 2 hours. Two-hour marathon meetings are (I'm sure you would agree)

In the student conference, the advocate and student develop a list of possible interventions.

To be effective, meetings should focus on goals and action plans and avoid discussing problems.

generally not a good expense of time, and they are usually counterproductive. In these long meetings, a majority of the time is usually taken up by hashing and rehashing the problem. I have seen far too many of these meetings adjourn without a substantive action plan. The RTI model in general, and the action-only meeting in particular, is designed to prevent everyone involved from spinning their wheels in this way.

The agenda for most action-only meetings goes something like this:

Introductions and focus on the DATA goal	2 minutes
Brainstorm everyone's ideas	12 minutes
Select ideas for further action	3 minutes
Explain a data collection technique	2 minutes
Set a time for the follow-up meeting	1 minute

During the meeting, team members post their ideas on a chart that is visible to everyone. This can be done traditionally (on paper or chalkboard) or electronically (projected from a computer). Figure 7.5 illustrates a typical brainstorming chart that is used in action-only meetings.

When the brainstorming session is over, the student chooses the one item from the "Student Ideas" list that he or she believes will work best. This commitment, made in front of the group, helps the student feel empowered over his or her own destiny while, at the same time, it requires the student to assume responsibility for his or her own growth. The parent and the teacher then follow suit and select their own strategies from the "Home Ideas" and "School Ideas" columns, respectively. Don't worry if the student and parent do not select a research-based intervention—only the teacher is responsible for that. Also, the sentiment that "There is nothing up there I like" shouldn't be a concern since each team member contributed at least one of the ideas on the board.

Figure 7.5	**Suggested Template for Recording Brainstorming Ideas**		
Home Ideas	**School Ideas**	**Student Ideas**	**Community**
1. Help Sonya set weekly goals. 2. Let her choose 6 math problems to do out of the 10 assigned. 3. Make up a "stump the students" question as homework to earn a homework pass. 4. Help her chart what she earns doing chores.	1. Build reflection time into every lesson. 2. Apply the stop-and-reflect reading strategy. 3. Add the teacher's notes to Sonya's notes to help her study. 4. Teach the SQ3R method. 5. Use graphic organizers for prewriting. 6. Have an aide work with Sonya in study hall to complete homework.	1. Tell the main idea to a partner before writing notes. 2. Draw symbols next to key ideas in notes. 3. Graph progress for words written per minute. 4. Practice writing six lines in four minutes about science class material. Count words daily.	1. Public librarian will help Sonya learn to use the services there. 2. Lion's Club will be asked for assistance with new glasses.

In all the years I have used this model, only once has it failed to result in an action plan that people felt responsible for and committed to. This one time was the result of a father who came to the meeting with an agenda to air his personal grievances about a teacher. I tried to redirect him by saying, "I can see you have an issue that is bothering you, but I am going to ask one favor. Can we first develop a plan for helping your daughter and then discuss the issue that is upsetting you?" He very colorfully refused, so we adjourned the meeting to another day so I could talk with him about his complaint. The message of this story is, do not allow anyone—parent or staff member—to divert the conversation away from constructive ideas focused on achieving the student's goals, even if you need to reschedule the meeting.

Conduct the follow-up meeting

Lack of follow-through was a major problem with the old intervention models. Teams would meet and people would make genuine commitments to action plans, but as soon as they walked down the hall, a hundred other problems started appearing, and the action plan quickly fell off the radar. In order for the plan to succeed, there must be a clear plan to monitor for fidelity of implementation.

The RTI coach generally is assigned some responsibility for touching base with the teacher between meetings to make sure data collection is proceeding according to plan. Principals also know which teachers are most likely to "drop the ball" and potentially forget to adhere to the plan. An important administrative responsibility is to visit teachers and regularly ask to see student data, especially for those students involved in the formal problem-solving process.

Follow-up meetings follow the same agenda as the initial meetings, except the first agenda item is different. These meetings provide an opportunity to share data collected by the parent, the student, and the teacher since the previous meeting. Each team member reports out, and the decision-making process begins. If the data points are above the goal lines on the progress monitoring chart, the team decides to do one of three things:

- Return the student to Tier 1 instruction, and monitor him or her for a few more weeks to ensure progress doesn't reverse.
- Gradually release the student from the extra services, and monitor the results.
- Continue the successful action plan for a few more weeks, and meet again to see if it is time to lessen the supplemental support.

Often, when students are successful with the new support program, parents and teachers are reluctant to let go of that extra service when it is no longer needed. In the long run, this is a disservice to the student because it can result in learned helplessness. This is almost as bad as not giving service at all because it not only restricts a student's potential for learning but also erodes self-confidence and motivation.

If the student's scores do not show sufficient (or any) growth, the team then asks three different questions:

1. Did we give the plan enough time to work?
2. Did we choose appropriate strategies?
3. Did we identify the right DATA goal?

Once the team is satisfied with answers to these questions, appropriate adjustments should be made, and the team should set a new follow-up meeting date. Many teachers ask, "How long do you keep this up?" The answer is "Until the student closes the gap or graduates from your school, whichever comes first." There is no point at which we give up. In a well-structured RTI framework, there is always another expert or team who can help generate new ideas and supports for students who struggle or for teachers who are at a loss for what to do next.

Summary

The problem-solving process can be used with large groups (districts or schools), small groups (grades or classrooms), or individual students.

1. Identify the problem and the desired outcome. The problem must focus on teachable skills that are within the school's sphere of influence.
2. Analyze why the problem is occurring. This is done using the "five reasons" process and by collecting data to verify possible causes of the original concern.

3. Form a hypothesis about what it will take to improve results, based on known information, possible causes, and progress-monitoring results.

4. Set a clear and measurable DATA goal, based on the hypothesis.

5. Select and implement research-based interventions and accommodations.

6. Evaluate the effectiveness of the intervention plan to see if the student is showing growth.

Teachers and parents need support to get used to this positive model of problem solving. It is easy to fall back on the old "gripe and go" model of family conferences. Though I have always been a proponent of the positive approach, it wasn't until I experienced an IAT as a parent that I understood the power of the positive and the damage of the negative. Involving the student and family as part of the decision-making team isn't just a polite formality. It is essential to effective change.

8

Compassionate and Competent Education

"Life is not about waiting for the storms to pass . . . it's about learning to dance in the rain."

—Anonymous

During my career, I was trained to individualize, differentiate, authentically assess, and curriculum map. I have been inclusioned and teamed, open-spaced and multiaged. They were worthy ideas that were tried, found to be difficult, and then abandoned, only to rise again with a new spin. Through the years, master teaching has held to the same core principles, and within this core is the essence of what students need and RTI requires. This is what compassionate and competent RTI teaching is all about.

As a principal and a supervisor, I repeatedly learned that when I lost my focus as a leader, the entire group lost steam. I had to stay on top of the latest research so I knew if we were offering the best strategies in our classrooms. I had to constantly be on guard against attractive opportunities that would distract us from our overall goals. I had to make certain that the professional development we offered was practical, proven, and would immediately make a difference in the classrooms.

When you are first getting started with RTI, you may ask, "How much work is this going to be?" My response is "How many of its components (assessment, pyramid, and problem solving) do you already know and use?" If you're spending an inordinate amount of time extinguishing academic and behavioral fires, then it's probably time to do some fire prevention. RTI assessment components help you know where to spend your time and resources. It takes a long time to learn how to operate efficiently if each teacher and administrator has to work independently and in isolation. You need to work in teams.

I can remember my feeling when I was assigned to my first classroom. I was in utter amazement that I was finally a teacher doing what I always wanted to do. Every day, my 2nd graders bounced into class and were ready to take on the world. I quickly learned that it takes a serious amount of energy and a considerable variety of strategies to keep that bounce from fading. A team of experts available for planning and collaboration certainly would have lightened that task. A good RTI structure provides exactly that.

I later moved to a kindergarten class and learned that classroom management is analogous to keeping smoke in a box. I had to develop clear and predictable routines. I had to be consistent in following through with rules and procedures if I wanted an effective learning atmosphere. A mentor to model strategies and help me through the rough spots would have been much appreciated. In districts with well-implemented RTI programs, this person is available as part of the expert pool.

As a 1st grade teacher, I learned that grouping the lowest-performing children together in one room is a cruel trick on both the teacher and the students. I had an opportunity to learn that lesson again as a special education teacher in the upper grades, but, thankfully, I had learned from my previous experiences. I partnered with a general education teacher, and we neutralized the stigmas on and isolation felt by those children. Together, we more than doubled the number of ideas for teaching all students at all levels. This would have been standard procedure in an RTI district, and the plan would have been a lot more sophisticated than the one we devised.

I eventually taught every grade K–6 and found each level to be exciting and exhausting in very different ways. I discovered that strategies that worked well in one grade generally worked just as well in another, with only a slight adjustment. In an RTI building, I would have had a bank of research-based ideas at my fingertips to expand my options.

When I tried my hand at 7th and 8th grade science, I experienced "culture shock" in the form of a boy named David. Many teachers have their own "David." These students either make you a more caring and competent teacher, or drive you away from the profession entirely.

David was a 16-year-old 8th grader with an attitude the size of Texas. From the very beginning, he informed me that he would not be doing anything related to science. I was taken aback and more than a little incensed at his gall. Like most early-career teachers, I took this as a personal challenge of my authority. I was certainly not going to put up with this.

David and I proceeded to go to war over his attitude. He soon became the daily talk of the teachers lounge. Teachers who knew him from previous years told one horror story after another about how impossible he was. Finally, some of the talk turned to why David was so angry. At the time, no one knew that David had witnessed a terrible tragedy while in 1st grade or that he had lived in an orphanage where they beat him regularly. We only knew that both in and out of school, David struck out at the world only to find that the world packed a heavier punch when it hit back. The stories went on and on about how he was detentioned, spanked, suspended, expelled, and put into juvenile detention centers. David was shuffled around with alarming regularity, and, through it all, no one seemed to notice that he could neither read nor write.

Once I saw the situation for what it was, David became a personal project. How could I make demands on a boy who couldn't comply even if he wanted to? It's probably fair to say that we made each other's lives a living hell while we ironed out an acceptable process for moving forward. Eventually, we gained mutual respect. By the end of the year, his attempts at the work were light-years ahead of his stubborn refusals at the beginning of the year.

I learned more about being a real teacher from David than I did in all the courses and seminars I ever attended. David taught me that students who don't feel safe and welcome in a classroom will not learn. Instead, they will either shut down or act out. If you don't take the time to learn the root cause of their problems, you will, in all likelihood, draw the wrong conclusions. I learned that I need to check my facts before I assume that a student is capable of doing the work. I learned that strategies that always work for most students might never work for others. As such, I learned that I needed to constantly upgrade and refine the tools of my trade. I also learned that no teacher is wise enough or strong enough to meet the needs of all the different types of kids entrusted to us, but if we put our hearts, talents, and heads together, there is no student we cannot teach.

Educators working as a compassionate and dedicated team can make the difference for every "David" we teach and for all the students who are much more fortunate. RTI is the support system that enables teachers to work as a team with continuous improvement. RTI is the right thing to do.

References

Access Center. (2004, October 1). *Concrete-representational-abstract instructional approach.* Available: http://www.k8accesscenter.org/training_resources/CRA_Instructional_Approach.asp

Barr, R. D., & Parrett, W. H. (2007). *The kids left behind: Catching up the underachieving children of poverty.* Bloomington, IN: Solution Tree.

Batch, G., Elliot, J., Graden, J., Grimes, J., Kovaleski, J., Prasse, D., Reschly, D., Schrag, J., Tilly, W. D. (2006). *Response to intervention: Policy considerations and implementation.* Alexandria, VA: National Association of State Directors of Special Education.

Bonwell, C. C., &. Eison, J. A. (1991). *Active learning: Creating excitement in the classroom.* San Francisco: Jossey-Bass.

Brophy, J., & McCaslin, M. (1992). Teachers' reports of how they perceive and cope with problem students. *Elementary School Journal, 93*(1), 3–68.

Burns, M. K. (2005). Using incremental rehearsal to increase fluency of single-digit multiplication facts with children identified as learning disabled in mathematics computation. *Education and Treatment of Children, 28,* 237–249.

Cherry, G., Ioannidou, A., Rader, C., Brand, C., & Repenning, A. (1999, June). *Simulations for lifelong learning.* Paper presented at the National Educational Computing Conference, Atlantic City, NJ.

Clowes, G. A. (2002, May). What characterizes an effective teacher? An exclusive interview with Barak Rosenshine. *The Heartland Institute School Reform News.* Available: http://www.heartland.org/policybot/results/9231/What_Characterizes_an_Effective_Teacher_an_exclusive_interview_with_Barak_Rosenshine.html

Deshler, D., Schumaker, J., Bulgren, J., Lenz, K., Jantzen, J., Adams, G., . . . Marquis, J. (2001). Making learning easier: Connecting new knowledge to things students already know. *TEACHING Exceptional Children, 33*(4), 82–85.

DeZure, D., Kaplan, M., & Deerman, M. (2001). *Research on student notetaking: Implications for faculty and graduate student instructors* (CRLT Occational Paper No. 16). Ann Arbor, MI: Center for Research on Learning and Teaching, University of Michigan.

Espin, C. (2009, May 8). Re: Curriculum-based measurement [Online forum comment]. Available: http://www.teachingld.org/expert_connection/cbm.html

Fuchs, L. S. (1991). Effects of curriculum-based measurement and consultation on teacher planning and student achievement in mathematics operations. *American Educational Research Journal, 28*(3), 617–641.

Fuchs, L. S., & Fuchs, D. (2009). *CBM modules: Using CBM in a response to intervention framework.* Available: http://www.rti4success.org/index.php?id=1172&Itemid=150&option=com_content&task=view

Gardill, M. C., & Jitendra, A. K. (1999). Advanced story map instruction: Effects on the reading comprehension of students with learning disabilities. *Journal of Special Education, 33*(1), 2–17, 28.

Ginsberg, M. B., & Wlodkowski, R. J. (2000). *Creating highly motivating classrooms for all students: A schoolwide approach to powerful teaching with diverse learners.* San Francisco: Jossey-Bass.

Glasser, W. (1992). *The quality school: Managing students without coercion* (2nd ed.). New York: Harper Perennial.

Good, R. H., & Jefferson, G. (1998). Contemporary perspectives on curriculum-based measurement validity. In M. R. Shinn (Ed.),

Advanced applications of curriculum-based measurement (pp. 61–88). New York: The Guilford Press.

Greene, R. W. (2008). *Lost at school: Why our kids with behavioral challenges are falling through the cracks and how we can help them.* New York: Scribner.

Harrison, M., & Harrison, B. (1986). Developing numeration concepts and skills. *Arithmetic Teacher, 33*(6), 18–21, 60.

Hayes-Jacobs, H. (2006). *Active literacy across the curriculum: Strategies for reading, writing, speaking, and listening.* Larchmont, NY: Eye on Education.

Hoover, J. J., Baca, L., Wexler-Love, E., & Saenz, L. (2008, August). *National implementation of response to intervention (RTI): Research summary.* Available: http://www.nasdse.org/Portals/0/NationalImplementationofRTI-ResearchSummary.pdf

Hosp, M. K., Hosp, J. L., & Howell, K. L. (2007). *The ABCs of CBM: A practical guide to curriculum-based measurement.* New York: The Guilford Press.

Hughes, C., Copeland, S. R., Agran, M., Wehmeyer, M. L., Rodi, M. S., & Presley, J. A. (2002). Using self-monitoring to improve performance in general education high school classes. *Education and Training in Mental Retardation and Developmental Disabilities, 37*(3), 262–272.

Hyerle, D. (1996). *Visual tools for constructing knowledge.* Alexandria, VA: ASCD.

Jensen, E. (1995). *Brain-based learning & teaching.* Del Mar, CA: Turning Point Publishing.

Kohl, H. R. (1994). *"I won't learn from you": And other thoughts on creative maladjustment.* New York: The New Press.

Linan-Thompson, S., & Vaughn, S. (2007). *Research-based methods of reading instruction for English language learners.* Alexandria, VA: ASCD.

Marzano, R. J. (2007). *The art and science of teaching: A comprehensive framework for effective instruction.* Alexandria, VA: ASCD.

Marzano, R. J. (2008). *Vision document.* Bloomington, IN: Marzano Research Laboratory.

Marzano, R. J., Marzano, J. S., & Pickering, D. J. (2003). *Classroom management that works: Research-based strategies for every teacher.* Alexandria, VA: ASCD.

Marzano, R. J., Pickering, D. J., & Pollock, J. E. (2001). *Classrom instruction that works: Research-based strategies for increasing student achievement.* Alexandria, VA: ASCD.

McKenzie, J. (2000). *Beyond technology: Questioning, research, and the information literate school.* Santa Barbara, CA: Linworth Publishing.

Merkely, D. M., & Jefferies, D. (2001). Guidelines for implementing a graphic organizer. *Reading Teacher, 54*(4), 350–357.

National Research Center on Learning Disabilities. (2007, Winter). SLD identification overview: General information and tools to get started. Available: http://www.nrcld.org/resource_kit/tools/SLDOverview2007.pdf

Peters, D. (1972). Effects of note taking and rate of presentation on short-term objective test performance. *Journal of Educational Psychology, 63*(3), 276–280.

Pitler, H., Hubbell, E. R., Kuhn, M., & Malenoski, K. (2007). *Using technology with classroom instruction that works.* Alexandria, VA: ASCD.

Powell, S., & Nelson, B. (1997). Effects of choosing academic assignments on a student with attention deficit hyperactivity disorder. *Journal of Applied Behavior Analysis, 30*(1), 185–186.

Purkey, W. W., & Novak, J. M. (1996). *Inviting school success: A self-concept approach to teaching, learning, and democratic practice.* Belmont, CA: Wadsworth.

Reeves, D. B. (2006). *The learning leader: How to focus school improvement for better results.* Alexandria, VA: ASCD.

Sanders, W. L., & Rivers, J. C. (1996). *Cumulative and residual effects of teachers on future student academic achievement.* Knoxville, TN: University of Tennessee Value-Added Research and Assessment Center.

Schunk, D. H. (1997, March). *Self-monitoring as a motivator during instruction with elementary school students.* Paper presented at the Annual Meeting of the American Educational Research Association, Chicago, IL.

Searle, M. A. (2004). *Standards-based instruction for all learners: A treasure chest for principal-led building teams in improving results for
learners most at-risk.* Columbus, OH: Ohio Department of Education.

Searle, M. A. (2007). *What to do when you don't know what to do: Building
a pyramid of interventions.* Perrysburg, OH: Searle Enterprises Inc.

Silberglitt, B., Burns, M. K., Madyun, M. H., & Lail, K. E. (2006).
Relationship of reading fluency assessment data with state
accountability test scores: A longitudinal comparison of grade
levels. *Psychology in the Schools, 43*(5), 527–535.

Smith, R. (2004). *Conscious classroom management: Unlocking the secrets
of great teaching.* Fairfax, CA: Conscious Teaching Publications.

Stecker, P. M., Fuchs, L. S., & Fuchs, D. (2005). Using curriculum-
based measurement to improve student achievement: Review of
research. *Psychology in the Schools, 42*(8), 795–819.

U.S. Department of Education, National Mathematics Advisory Panel.
(2008). *Foundations for success: The final report of the National
Mathematics Advisory Panel.* Available: http://www.ed.gov/about/
bdscomm/list/mathpanel/report/final-report.pdf

U.S. Department of Health and Human Services, National Institutes of
Health, National Institute of Child Health and Human Development.
(2000). *Teaching children to read: An evidence-based assessment of
the scientific research literature on reading and its implications for
reading instruction: Reports of the subgroups.* Report of the National
Reading Panel (NIH Publication No. 00-4754). Washington, DC: U.S.
Government Printing Office.

Van der Klift, E., & Kunc, N. (2009). *The human service system: Pyramid
or circle?* Available: http://www.normemma.com/advocacy/arsys-
tem.htm

VanDerHeyden, A. (2005). *Using RTI to improve learning in mathematics.*
Available: http://www.rtinetwork.org/Learn/Why/ar/RTIandMath/1

Wenglinsky, H. (1998). *Does it compute? The relationship between
educational technology and student achievement in mathematics.*
Available: http://ets.org/Media/Research/pdf/PICTECHNOLOG.pdf

Wiggins, G., & McTighe, J. (2005). *Understanding by design* (2nd ed.).
Alexandria, VA: ASCD.

Wilhelm, J. (2001). *Improving comprehension with think-aloud strategies: Modeling what good readers do.* New York: Scholastic Professional Books.

Willis, J. (2006). *Research-based strategies to ignite student learning.* Alexandria, VA: ASCD.

Willis, J. (2007). *Brain-friendly strategies for the inclusion classroom.* Alexandria, VA: ASCD.

Wolfe, P. (2001). *Brain matters: Translating research into classroom practice.* Alexandria, VA: ASCD.

Wormeli, R. (2005). *Summarization in any subject.* Alexandria, VA: ASCD.

Index

Note: the letter *f* following a page number denotes a figure.

About the Author

Margaret A. Searle is the president of Searle Enterprises, Inc., an educational consulting firm. She specializes in consulting with districts and schools in the areas of curriculum alignment, differentiated instruction, inclusive education, leadership team development, and training teams to implement RTI. She also serves as an adjunct professor for Ashland University in Ashland, Ohio. Her teaching experience covers every grade from preschool through 8th grade in both a general and special education capacity. Her administrative experience has been as a K–12 supervisor in Dayton City Schools as well as a middle school principal in Springfield, Ohio, and an elementary school principal in Toledo, Ohio. She served as an advisor to President George H. W. Bush on elementary and secondary education issues.

Margaret has written two previous books, *Standards-Based Instruction for All Learners: A Treasure Chest for Principal-Led*

Building Teams and *What to Do When You Don't Know What to Do: Building a Pyramid of Interventions*. Margaret is based in Perrysburg, Ohio, and can be contacted through her Web site: www.margaretsearle.com; by e-mail: searle@buckeye-express. com; or by phone: (419) 874-9505.

Related ASCD Resources

At the time of publication, the following ASCD resources were available (ASCD stock numbers appear in parentheses). For up-to-date information about ASCD resources, go to www.ascd.org. You can search the complete archives of *Educational Leadership* at www.ascd.org/el.

Networks

Visit the ASCD Web site (www.ascd.org) and search for "networks" for information about professional educators who have formed groups around topics like "Assessment for Learning," "Interdisciplinary Curriculum and Instruction," and "Quality Education." Look in the "Network Directory" for current facilitators' addresses and phone numbers.

Print Products

The Art and Science of Teaching: A Comprehensive Framework for Effective Instruction by Robert J. Marzano (#107001)

Collaborative Analysis of Student Work: Improving Teaching and Learning by Georgea M. Langer, Amy Bernstein Colton, Loretta S. Goff (#102006)

Educating Everybody's Children: Diverse Teaching Strategies for Diverse Learners (revised and expanded 2nd edition) edited by Robert W. Cole (#107003)

Educational Leadership October 2007 Early Intervention at Every Age (#108021)

Enhancing RTI: How to Ensure Success with Effective Classroom Instruction and Intervention by Douglas Fisher, Nancy Frey (#110037)

Getting to "Got It!": Helping Struggling Students Learn How to Learn by Betty K. Garner (#107024)

Reframing Teacher Leadership to Improve Your School by Douglas B. Reeves (#108012)

Videos

Breaking Through Barriers to Achievement (#605133)

How to Informally Assess Student Learning (#605121)

Implementing RTI in Secondary Schools (#610011)

THE WHOLE CHILD The Whole Child Initiative helps schools and communities create learning environments that allow students to be healthy, safe, engaged, supported, and challenged. To learn more about other books and resources that relate to the whole child, visit www.wholechildeducation.org.

For more information: send e-mail to member@ascd.org; call 1-800-933-2723 or 703-578-9600, press 2; send a fax to 703-575-5400; or write to Information Services, ASCD, 1703 N. Beauregard St., Alexandria, VA 22311-1714 USA.